Recipes from John Crophill's Commonplace Book

Edited by

Daniel Myers

CONTENTS

INTRODUCTION

The text known as Harley MS 1735 a handwritten manuscript in Latin and Middle English, containing entries on a wide range of subjects. It is currently held at the British Library. The manuscript was assembled by John Crophill, a medical practitioner and bailiff of Wix Priory in Essex, sometime before his death in 1485. Images of the original manuscript are freely available on the British Library website.

The sixty-nine culinary recipes included here appear together in a small section (ff. 16v-28v) of the first volume of the manuscript. In addition to the full text of these recipes, I've included related recipes from contemporary English sources, with special attention to those appearing in *Liber Cure Cocorum* (Sloane MS 1986) and *A Noble Boke off Cookry* (Holkham MSS 674), which appear to be more closely related than the other sources.

My goal in creating this transcription was to make the recipes widely available to food historians in a usable form. I have done my best to provide an accurate, but readable transcription. Common abbreviations have been expanded, the letters thorn and yogh have been replaced with their modern equivalents, and some minor punctuation has been added.

1

THE TEXT

[the recipes begin on f.16v]

[1] A Tarte of Fysch
Tak fygges & reysingis & cyng[?] [f.17r] hem & do ther to freysch samoun or othyr maner of freysch fysch grynd alle to gyder temper hem up with almounde mylk & frye almounds in swete oyle & do therinne lye alle to gydr do ther to pouder of galingale reysings of coraunce quybybes & soden perys & schere hem & cast hem ther inne amonge alle to gidre & of ilk of the spyces kepe the halvendel with outen colour thi fars with saffroun & swet it with sugre. Tak laumpreys & laumprouws & elys & dares & roches & loches smeltys and other maner of freysch fysch & wete hem in flour frye hem in swete oyle & loke thu have dats farsed & plumbys damaycynis than go to the ovene & mak dowe & couche thi fars on this maner, fferst ley thi kake of dowe than tak thi fars & couche thi fryed fysch & thi dats farsed & plumbys & thi almondys & drengle it in swete oyle & poudre it with sugre & lay thou thi fars on this [f.17v] maner couche thi fars as thu wylt have hulke it & pinche it & mak thi lowes colour it with saffron & set it inne the ovene & yf you wylt hawe of foure coliurs make it as I have tawte of the tou or of the tothere.

[2.] Browet of Almayne
Tak almonde melk lye it with amydon ore with bake flour colour it with saffron force it with good pouder of ginger & canel & galingale. Tak parterkes & chykenes & hewe hem on quarterrys do the melk over the feyre & boylle it do in thi fleysch seson it with sugre.

[3.] Furmente
Tak whete & pike it fayre do it in a morter stampe it alitel &
sprenkle it with water stampe it hol waysche it fayre do it in a pot
boille it tyl it breste set it doun & tak cow melk playe it up with
alytyl tyl it be thykke lye it up with yolkys of ayren colour it with
saffron kep it wel fro brennynge.

[4.] Blamanger
Tak rys & waysch hem & drye hem & tempre hem up with
almonde melk. Tak broyn of caponis or of hennys [f.18r] good
plente & tose it smal do the rys & the melk to gydre ovr the feyr
boylle charche it with the tosed fleysch seson it with sugre
florysche the dysch with fryed almondys.

[5.] Chaudon Sauz of Swannes
Tak the issu of the swannes & wasch hem wel skoure the guttys
with salt sethz al to gidre. Tak of the fleysch hewe it smal & the
guttys with alle. Tak bred gynger & galingale canel grynd it &
tempre it up with bred colour it with blood or with brent bred
seson it up with a lytyl vinegre welle it al to gydere.

[6.] Amydone
Take whete & step it ix days & chaunche the water every day twyes
brose it in a morter rythe smal tempre it up sithen with melk or
water sye it thorow an harsine let it stonde stylle til it be stable
poure out the water ley it on a cloghet turne it til it be bon drye.

[7.] Conyes in Grave
Take conyes & sethz hem wel tak hem up & wasch hem in cold
water tak melk of almonds lyze it up with [f.18v] amydon or with
myed bred force it up with ginger & with clowes boille it on the
fyer hew the conyes & do ther to seson it up with wyn & sugre.

[8.] Chikens in Cryteyne
Tak cowys melk lye it up with amydon or with flour force it up
with poudre of ginger galentyn canel comyn colour it up with
saffron sethz the chikenis hew hem on quarters boille it alle to
gidre seson it up with sugre.

[9.] Viaunde de Cipre

4

Tak braun of capouns or of hennis dryve hem hew hem smal braye hem in a morter as smal as myed bred tak good almonde mylk lye it up with amydon or with flour of rys colour it with saffron charche it with brayed fleysch seson it with sugre florysch it with clowes & maces.

[10.] Maretrel de le Char
Tak hennes flesch & pork & sethz to gidre tak it up & pyk outh the bonys hewe it smale grynd wel kast it ageyn in to the brothz charge it with myed wastel bred colour it with saffron [f.19r] boylle it & gwan it is boylled set it of the fyr lye it with yelkys eyren florysch the dysch with poudre.

[11.] Chaudone Potage of Pygys
Tak the hert the lunge the lyvore the mydre the guttis skoure the guttys with salt seth hem hew hem smal tak pepyr & bred grounde to gydre tempre it up with brothz colour it up with blood lye it with yelkys of eyren yf thou do yt to browes colour it with saffron.

[12.] Browes de Chaudoun
Tak flour & yelkys of eyren mak past mak pelets smal frye hem in oyle de oyle and in sugre or in freysch gres do in the past aparty of the pouder.

[13.] Noumbles of Net
Tak the hert & the kedneye & the myd dredde hew smal as deys presse hem wel sethz hem in water & in god ale colour it with brent brede ferce it with pouder of peper & canel sethz it ovir the feyr & boylle it seson it with vinegre or eysel.

[14.] Roo in [f.19v] Sewe
Tak a roo & pyke it clene & perboille it & tak it up & drye it & hewe it on smale gobets do it in a pot kast him ther to bylle it well & boille it force it with good pouder & colour it with blod or saundres.

[15.] Counsis
Tak capouns hennys & rost hem tyl thei been browne hew hem on gobets do hem in a brothz of fresch beef sethz hem softly or sethz hem ferst & rost hem after on a gredel tak the brothz & lye it up

with bred force it with peper colour it with saffron sethz eyre hard
kepe the yelkys hole hew the whyte smal & do ther to and do ther
to the brothz & the capouns hew hem ther to boille it & set it
doun seson it with yelkys swenged florysch it with hard
yelkys & hole.

[16.] Let Lorres des Aguellys
Tak elys & culpon hem & sethz hem seke dely tak out the bonys &
saf the culpouns hole swenge eyren in a vessel & do ther to elys tak
melk & colour it with saffron [f.20r] fforce it with comyn & set it
to the feyr & quen it gynnit to welle do in the eyren & the elys stire
hem to gidre sethz hem til the krudden.

[17.] Cherise
Tak ripe cherise do out the stonis bray hem in a morter ryth wel tak
thykke almounde melk & tempre it up with al draw it thorw abultel
lye it with amydon or with flour of rye flerysch it with ginger or
galingale canel qwybibys & maces colour it with saffron seson it
with wyn & sugre.

[18.] Soppes Dorre
Tak minced onyowns & oyle de oyle & sethz hem to gidre sithen
tak wyn or ale & boille it ther with than tak tosted bred & poure
the sewe ther on & melk of almondys above.

[19.] Blawmanger of Lekys
Tak the whyte of lekys & sethz them longe in water & in vinegre &
hony waysch hem in many waterys presse hem in a clothz brest
hem in a morter tak rys & skerue hem temper [f.20v] hem up with
almonde melk boille it & lye it up with lekys florysch the dysch
with myed almondes & sugre.

[20.] Browet of Almayne
Loke thu have good ale & cler & seson it with qwyth bred melk of
almondys tak onyouns & mince hem and do al to the feyr & qwat
fleysch do thu haft do ther to rau after that it wil sethen tak clowes
& maces & qwybibes & do hem in hole & lat hem sethen & do to a
perty ginger & oatmel & if the colour be noth good as fallet to the
canel tak a perty saffron & mak the colour good & if it charge nowt
wel tak flour of rys & do ther to.

[21.] Rys Rayle
Tak sugre & whyt salt and broth & fyggys & fleysch of hennis &
pork & grynd hem wel to gidre tak bred & par awey the our kurste
& tak the togher kurst & grynd in stede of lyour & canel gynger &
a perty of galyngale grynd it & seson it so it charge wel the colour
sal ben of the selve.

[22.] Pochee
Tak fyggs [f.21r] & reysynggs & grynd hem wel & seson it with
good almonde mylk & do ther to agod porcion of canel & of
ginger & if it charge nowth tak flour of rys & do ther to tyl it be
wel stondynge than do to salt.

[23.] Browet Mese
Tak canel & ginger saffron & persely & grynd it & tempre it with
good broth tak eyren & brek hem & drawe hem thorow a cloth do
awey the strene tak sithen thin thre thingys & draw also do to the
feyr & qwan it wellith do ther to swich flesch as thu hast sodon &
than thin eyren after & whych salt.

[24.] Crane
Loke thu have good broth & cler & good blaunched almondys
grynd hem & tempre hem up with thin broth & drawe it hulle it
wel & do it on the fyer charge it wel with amydon or with flour of
rys do ther to qwyth ginger & a perty canel sugre qwybibes &
clowes a perty gres & salt.

[25.] Charlet Gentyl
Tak pork & grynd it with cow melk breke eyren & draw hem & do
ther to & saffron & grynd it [f.21v] al to gider seson it at the feyr &
sythen let resten a qwyle tak than a clene cloth & do it ther inne &
sye outh the iews tak sithen melk of almondys & ginger & galingale
& mak a sew chargeant as grave & do ther to sugre & clowes &
maces seson it wel do ther to qwyth salt tak sythen the charlet
outh of the cloth & schere it with a knyf on schywer & do ther to
the sew.

[26.] Viaunde de Cipre
Grynd almondys & tempre it up with good broth tak braun of

hennys & pork yef myst be hewe it and grynd it & seson it up
with flour of rys yt it be chargeaunt colour it with saffron thanne
do to sugre & ginger after it asket do ther to gres than do it fro the
fyer to reste.

[27.] Viaunde de Burgeoun
Tak good broth & the of the vine & mince & grynd it & tempre it
with broth & wyt mylk & win & drawe it thorow a cloth & tempre
thi fleysch ther with tak sythen flour of rys & do ther to so that it
be chargeaunt & do [f.22r] ther to canel & a perty greyn de pareys
& sugour & qwyth salt the colour sal ben fade grene.

[28.] Burgeoun de Vyne
Grynd almondys & tempre with broth & rys nouth over mychyl
skerved & tak the furthe of the vine long schorn in the maner of
braun of hennys welle hem do the rys & the mylk to gyder to the
fyer & qwan it is chargeaunt do in thin furches in the maner of
braun & do ther to sugre & salt.

[29.] Rys Camelyn
Tak rys nought over mychel skerved do it to the fyer with almonde
mylke let it well tyl it be chargeaunt & do ther to pouder of canel &
a perty of saffron & sugre & salt.

[30.] A Stywe
Tak afayr pot & do in gres and fleysch hylle it wel & do in good
poudre of ginger & of galingale & do in vyn & do it from the fyer
& cure if fro cold & do the to salt.

[31.] A Gelle
Tak gledes & bronnys & grete elys wel wasche & brothe & do to
the fyer to sethen & qwan it is soden tak the broth & do it to the
fyer & do to [f.22v] clowes gelofres gingour galingale broken but
nouth over muchel & saffron & qwan it is wel soden drawe it
thorow a cloth in to a vessel of tre & do the fysch in the broth &
cover it let it stonde & kelen the space of anyth for it sal ben served
cold & do the fysch in the same maner.

[32.] Garbage
Tak fleysch & wasch it & do it to the fyer take percely & brek yt

with thin honds & do in spices and saffron & wyn let it boyle wel
non other lite but salt.

[33.] Counses
Tak capouns & dysch hem to the fyer & qwan thei ben soden tak
bred & grynd it ther with & tempre it than do in spices and saffron
sethe eyren hard & tak the qwyte & mynce it & do it in let it wellen
take the yelkys of eyren & seson it ther with do to gres & salt &
qwan it sal ben served do the yelkys of the eyren in the disch.

[34.] Cyvee
Tak capouns & perboylle hem in good broth do hem in than to
rosten grynd bred [f.23r] tak spices & mak liour mynce onyons
smale & welle hem with qwyth gres do to yelkes of raw eyren seson
it al to gidre do to salt.

[35.] Rosee
Tak fleysch of hennys & pork & seth it & mak good broth & cler
tak levis of rosys wel lesyn & clene wasch hem & grynd hem &
tempre hem with the broth & do it to the fyer tak flour of rys or of
wastelbred mak it chargeaunt tak so then of the hole rosys and do
ther to & let it wellen tak a perty of saundrys and saffron to the
colour do to salt do it fro the fyer & qwan it sal ben dressed
strew in the disch of the levis of the rose as it were in the manere
of pouder.

[36.] Prymerose
Loke that thou have god broth & cler almondys grounen tempre it
with the broth & drawe it thorow a cloth tak floures of primrose &
do ther to & tak braun of hennys & hewe & grynd it & do ther
to & let it wellen & do ther to flour of rys tyl it be chargeaunt &
do ther to flowres of primerose & [f.23v] ginger & sugre and salt
& qwan is sal ben dressed ley on floures of primerose the maner
of spices.

[37.] Cewe de Kounsye
Tak beef & hew it samal scher it & do it to the feyr & grynd
garlic & do ther to & of the best spices & grynd bred & ly et in the
maner of noumbles do to salt & qwan it is wellyd do it from
the fyer.

[38.] Farsure of Wych
Tak fys[che] [al as?] beste and yelkys of eyren soden & saffron gynd eyren raw & bred poudre & sugre as be farse.

[39.] Tarts of Flesch
Tak fleysch of capouns or of hennys & pork & fyggys & reysings & eyren hard soden wel gronden alle to gidre brod & raw eyren do to saffron & pouder of ginger & canel and galingale & sugre & do ther to clowes & maces hole than make thin cofyn & do a cours of fleysch of perterkys or of ploverys or other volatyl al hewy & nother cours of the grounde mete & menge it togider. [f.24r]

[40.] Mawmene
Tak a pond of sugre & a qwart of water & an half & do it in a pot with sugre & tak amydoun & lye it ther with & tak a tendre chese & grynd it in a morter & tempre it up with almounde melk & do it in a pot & set it on the fyer & styre it wele & tak fleysch of chykenys & hew & grynd it & tempre it up with almaunde melk wel thykke & qwan thi pot is wel boylled tak it of the fyer & lye it up with fleysch & do ther to god poudre of ginger or of canel & wyth grece & dresse it & plant it.

[41.] Browet of Sarasynes
Tak crustes of qwyt bred & blood & do it in a morter & grynd it & tempre it with swet broth & draw it thorow a cloth & do it in a pot & do ther in red wyn set it on the fyer & lye it & boylle it tak perterkes & wodekokes & other smale brydes & rost hem & qwirter hem & do hem in a pot & do ther to god poudre of clowes & qwybybes & sugre & sethz it do ther in wyth grece & tast it & [f.24v] dresse it.

[42.] Browet Seche
Tak capouns or conyes & hew hem on gobets & waysch hem & do hem in a pot tak persoly & sauge & onyons & hew hem alle to gidre do it in a pot & red wyne & switch broth half of the ton & half of the tother & do it in the pot so that the fleysch be twey fynger brede above the pot & do ther to hol saffron & bylle it wel that non brethz go outh & set on the fyer & do ther to wyth gres &

10

good poudere of galyngale clowes & qwybibes & let it sethen anow
than do ther in sugre & dresse it.

[43.] Browet Ingse
Tak good galentyn & tempre it up weth broth & drawe it thow a
fayer cloth do it in a pot & set it on the fyer. Tak qwayles & yonge
pertrikes & qwarter hem & do hem in a pot & set the pot on the
fyer & stire it wel & do ther in good pouder of galentyn & wyth
gres & clowes & qwybibes & let it se then tyl the fleys is
sodden anow tak it than of the fyer & dresse it & pouder it with
sugre & maces.

[44.] Blaunch Desorre
Mak [f.25r] gode melk of swete almaundes & skerve the rys & do
hem in a morter & grynd hem & tempre hem up with almaunde
melk & draw it thorow a cloth & do it in a pot & set it on the fyer
& stire it wel tak braun of capouns & do awey the skyn & the
bonys & hewe it & grynd it & tempre it up with wyn & wan thi pot
hayth wel boylled do ther inne of wyth ginger & tak it fro the fyer
& lye it with grounde fleysch & do ther inne qwyth salt & sugre &
tast it & loke that it be owerte of savour & poynaunt of the wyth
ginger & loke that the thre savours a cor den ilk with othyr &
dresse it & plante it with poumgarnett & gelofres.

[45.] Freschure
Tak the hert & the lyver & the blood of the hydes & sethz hem &
hewe hem in a pot & do ther to qwyth gres & frye it & tak the
blood & grynd it in a morter & tempre it up with red wyn & do it
in the pot & tak myed bred & grynd it & tempre it up with aly tyl
swet broth & lye it ther with wel chargeaunt [f.25v] & do ther inne
good pouder & sugre florysch & serve it forth.

[46.] Apilmows de Gesse
Tak apyllys & seth hem & grynd hem & drawe hem thorow a
cloth & do hem in a pot & do ther to melk of almaunds & set it on
the fyer & qwan it is boylled do ther to a good perty of wyth gres &
loke that thu have many yelkys of eyren & do ther to in a good
perty of sugre colour it with saffron dresse it & poudre it
with sugre.

[47.] (untitled)
Tak freysch pork hew it & grynd it smal tak yelkys of eyren grind hem & do ther to good ginger galingale do ther to tak maces & qwybibes & clowes do ther to al hole & sugre & poudre gret plente than ley in the cofyn a smal couche of farsure tak perterkes & chikenys & hew hem on qwarter & frye hem & smale bryddys al hole fryed and conyes & do ther to a good bundel of fleysch than ley on farsure a nother good couche & do therin & do ther in greyn de parys & qwybibes & clowes & est ley a nother couche [f.26r] of farsure cvre it with past colour it wyt yelkys of eyren.

[48.] A Tarte Pernusames
Tak fresch pork & sethz it & do awey the skyn & the bonys & grynd it in a morter tak good chese & cyy it & tempre al to gidre than tempre it with eyren do therinne almaund fryede & good poudre of galingale & clowes & qwybibes & sugre & salt & saffron & reysings with out thu pepynes & grynd al to gidre tak perterkes & ploveres & wodekokes & other smale brydds tak conyes & kerwe hem & frye hem as was forseyd & farse thi dat & mak dow & couche the tarte thus ferst ley at the than aftyr ley thi farse & ley a perty of flesch ther inne & than qwibebes & sugre & good poudre reysings & dats & pumbys & damacyns & fryed almaunds ley al this in the tarte & ley thin oth couche on thi farse colour it with saffron mak thin lowes & set it in the ovene.

[49.] A Tarte of Fysche
Tak figgs & waysch hem & grynd hem [f.26v] smal tempre hem with vinegre tak freysch samoun haddokes perches & pykes tak out the bonys bray hem to gidre in a morter tak poudre of ginger & galingale & meng with al tak maces & qwybibes & clowes & do ther to al hole & sugre gret plente tak ther of & do in thi cofyn a smal couche tak elys & lamprouns and frye hem to gidre in oyle de oyle & lay ther in a couche of the brayed mete & do ther to botre of almaunde melk covere it with past colour it with inne & with outen.

[50.] Charlet
Tak swete melk & colour it with saffron tak freysch pork soden hewe it smal sweng eyren & cast alm the melk set it over the fyer boille it stere it wel to gider kele it with a lytyl ale & set it doun.

[51.] Ravioles
Tak freysch pork & braun of hennys grind it smal yelks of eyren &
grind hem & do ther to good poudre of maces qwybibes & mong
with alwynd it in past & set it in a panne of fat broth colour it with
saffron & florysch hem with hole chese [f.27r] gratyd.

[52.] Jussele
Mye wastelbred swenge eyren & do ther to tak good fat broth of
freysch beof colour it with saffron boille it al softely & in the
boyllingg do al this ther to & do to sauge & percyle.

[53.] Bokenande
Tak almaunde melk colour it with saffron forse it with good
poudre tak fat fleysch wel soden hew on smale gobets do ther to
lye it with amydon or with bake flour boille it set it don florysch it
with poudre.

[54.] Blaunde Sorre
Tak rys & wasch hem & grynd hem smal tempre hem up with
almaunde melk do it ovre the fyer & boylle it tak braun of hennys
& of capouns hew it & grynd it smal as myed bred do ther to seson
it with sugre gret plente florysch it with fryed almaunds.

[55.] Rosee
Tak flour of rys tempre it with almaunde melke lye it tyl it be
chargeaunt tak braun of caponys or of hennys hew it & grynd it
smal charge it with al colour it with alysaundre or with blood force
it with clowes & maces seson it with sugre [f.27v] gret plente.

[56.] Ynde de Cypres
It sal ben mad as blaunde sorre save the colour sal ben of ynde
bandas or of the flour of the violet.

[57.] Letlardes
Tak eryn & cow melk & swenge hem to gidre tak lard of freysch
pork & sithen schere it on smale pecys kast it ther in hoylle & styr
it tyl it be gaderyd on a crudde than leche it & kest it on a grederne
& serve it with frotours.

[58.] Botre of Almaunde Melk
Tak thykke almaunde melk boyle it & in the boylinge kast ther in
vinegre or vin do it sethen on a canwaas abred gadre it sethen on
an keep than hange it up on a cloth amylewey wyle ley it after in a
cold water than serve it forth.

[59.] Charlet Aforce
Tak cow melk & eyren & swenge hem to gidre & colour it with
saffron tak freysch pork hew it smal do it ther to kast it in a panne
boyle it wel & stire it vyn & with ale set it don than ley it on a
canwas presse out the wyth tak almaunde melk colour it with
saffron lye it with [f.28r] amydon force it with poudre of
ginger & galingale.

[60.] Farsure
Tak freysch pork soden hew it smal tak yelkes of eren & meng with
al force it with poudre swete it with sugre do ther to maces
qwibebis & clowes al hole colour it with saffron do it in the
chykennys than boyle hem & tak hem up rost hem with gres if it
be nede.

[61.] Farsure For Soper
Tak hard eyren soden & hew hem smal tak percyle & sauge & hew
it smal do ther to & do it in the chikenys.

[62.] Char de Marchaunt
Tak good moton hew it on gobets & set it in a pot tak brod peper
& percely grynd hem to gider tempre hem up with bred than do
ther to salt & welle it.

[63.] Powmes Dorre
Tak good farsure & mak balles do hem in a panne of clene water
boyle hem alityl tyl they begynng to swelle than tak hem up & ley
hem on a boord to dreyen tak yelkes of eyren of swenge hem wel
ther inne & let hem dreyen do hem on a spite & rost hem & in the
rostinge powre on [f.28v] the yelkys of eyren flawme hem with
grees serve hem forth with frytur.

[64.] Brewet Sechz
Hew moton & chykenys on morcellis & sethz hem with onyons & percely.

[65.] Brewet of Elys
Lye it with bred force it with poudre colour it with saffron.

[66.] Browet of Lamprouns
Lye it with bred force it with poudre of peper & galingale.

[67.] Perre
Draw soden perys thorow a sarce so hem in a vessel to freysch broth tak sugre & hony & do ther to freysch gres tak of capouns & of hennys grynd saml & meng with al kepe it wel fro brennyng kele it & lye it charge it with yelkys of eyren.

[68.] Maumene
Tak fyggys & reysings & lese hem & grind hem & good melk of almaundys & braun of capouns & of hennys nouth outhr in yche grounden for that sal ben the colour than do there to ginger clowes gelofres & greyn de parys & sugre & salt.

[69.] Kokeneye
Tak fleysch of hennys & of capouns & lene of pork & hew the ton with the tother & onyons mynced in the broth

NOTES ON THE RECIPES

1. A Tarte of Fysch

The final sentence of this recipe—instructing the cook to color the tart as described earlier—strongly suggests that it was copied from some other source as there are no preceding recipes to refer to.

There are many similar recipes for fish pies in the surviving medieval cookbooks, though I haven't found any that closely follow the one in *Crophill*.

> Tartes of Fyssche. Take Fygys, and Roysoynys, and pike an sethe in Wyne; than take Costardys, Perys, and pare hem clene, and pike out the core, and putte hem in a morter with the frute; then tak Codlyng or haddok, other Elys, and sethe hem and pike owt the bonys, and grynd alle y-fere, and do ther-to a lytel wyne, and melle to-gederys: an do ther-to Canelle, Clowys, Mace3, Quybibe3, pouder Gyngere, and of Galyngale, and pepir, and Roysonys of coraunce, and coloure it with Safroun. When thou makyst thin cofyns, than take gode fat Ele, and culpe hym, and take owt the stonys of Datys, and farce hem; and blaunche Almaundys, and caste ther-to; but fyrste frye hem in Oyle, and couche al this a-mong, and bete thin cofyns with the ledys, and bake, and serue forth. [Two Fifteenth-Century Cookery-Books (England, 1430)]

> CRUSTARDES OF FYSSHE. XX.VII. XVI. Take loches, laumprouns, and Eelis. smyte hem on pecys, and stewe hem wiþ Almaund Mylke and verions, frye the loches in oile as tofore. and lay þe fissh þerinne. cast þeron powdour fort powdour douce. with raysons coraunce & prunes damysyns.

take galyntyn and þe sewe þerinne, and swyng it togyder and cast in the trape. & bake it and serue it forth. [Forme of Cury (England, 1390)]

2. Browet of Almayne

There are numerous versions of this stew in other sources. The variations in the recipe's name are interesting in that they either to reflect the use of almond milk, or they imply a German origin (Allemagne is the French name for Germany).

The ingredients and the instructions to color the stew it with saffron make the following two recipes the closest match.

> To mak Bruet de almondes tak almond mylk and alay it with amydon or with whet flour bulted coloure it with saffron and fors it with pouder of ginger canelle and galingale then tak pertuche or chekens and sethe them and hew them in quarto and set the mylk on the fyere to boylle and florish it with pouders and serue it. [A Noble Boke off Cookry (England, 1468)]

> Breuet de almonde. Take gode almonde mylke anon, And loke þou lye hit with amydone, Or with flowre þat is bake. Coloure hit with safron, I undurtake. Fors hit with powder of þy male Of gyngere, canel, and galingale. Take pertrykes and chykyns and hom wele sethe. Hew hom in quarters fayre and smethe. Do þat mylke over þo fyre þat tyde, And boyle and sett hit doune besyde, And florysshe hit with powdur, as I þe kenne, Þou may have more menske emong alle menne. [Liber cure cocorum (England, 1430)]

3. Furmente

There are a number of different versions of frumenty in the surviving medieval cookbooks, but there are two which are reasonably similar. The unusual use of the word "play" in all three is especially worth noting, and could be a copy error for "alay".

To mak furmente tak whet and pik it clene and put it in a
mortair and bray it till it hull then wenowe it and wesshe it and
put it unto the pot and boile it till it brest then sett it down and
play it up with cow mylk till yt be enoughe alay it with yolks of
eggs and kep it that it byrn not, colour it with saffron do ther
to sugar and salt it and serue it. [A Noble Boke off Cookry
(England, 1468)]

Furmente. Take wete, and pyke hit fayre and clene And do hit
in a morter shene. Bray hit a lytelle, with water hit spryng Tyl
hit hulle, with-oute lesyng. Þen wyndo hit wele, nede þou mot.
Wasshe hit fayre, put hit in pot. Boyle hit tylle hit brest, þen
Let hit doun, as I þe kenne. Take know mylke, and play hit up
To hit be thykkerede to sup. Lye hit up with 3olkes of eyren,
And kepe hit wele, lest hit berne. Coloure hit with safron and
salt hit wele, And servyd hit forthe, Syr, at þe mele. With sugur
candy, þou may hit dowce, If hit be served in grete lordys
howce. Take black sugur for mener menne. Be ware þer with,
for hit wylle brenne. [Liber cure cocorum (England, 1430)]

4. Blamanger
There are numerous contemporary recipes for blancmanger, but
the closest appear to be the ones below.

Blonc Manger. Take ryse and loke þou wasshe hom clene, And
þorowgh a strynour þou hom strene. Temper hom with
almonde mylke anon. Take brawne of capons or henne good
won, Tese hit smalle, as I þe lere. Do þe ryse in þo mylke over
þe fyre, Let hit boyle for ony nede. Charge hit with tesyd
flesshe in dede. Seson hit with sugar, and floresshe With fryud
almondes þo lordes dysshe. [Liber cure cocorum (England,
1430)]

To mak blanche mange of flesshe tak ryse and wesshe it and
draw it throughe a stren and temper it with almond mylk then
teese the braun of capon or henn small and put the rise to the
mylke and boile it and charge it with the tosed flesshe sesson it
with sugur and florisshe it with almonds and serue it. [A Noble
Boke off Cookry (England, 1468)]

Given the number of parallels so far with *Liber Cure Cocorum*, I wonder if someone edited the recipes from that work to make them more readable by dropping the rhyming form.

5. Chaudon Sauz of Swannes

While there are similar recipes in many other sources, there are a couple that are notably close. It is especially interesting that both *Crophill* and *Noble* include the instruction to scour the guts with salt.

> To mak chaudron for swan wild duck or pigge take and wesshe the issus of a swan and skour the guttes with salt and sethe them to gedour and hewe small bothe the flesshes and the guttes and put ther to canelle or galingale put myed bred ther to and temper it with the brothe or with the blod and sesson it to venygar and boille them in a possuet and serue them furthe. [A Noble Boke off Cookry (England, 1468)]

> Sawce for swannus. Take þo offal and þo lyver of þo swan, In gode brothe þou sethe hom þan. When hit is sothyne, take oute þe bonus, Smalle hew þo flesshe, Syr, for þe nonus. Make alyoure of crust of brede, Of blode of swanne, þat soþun is lede, Caste powdur of gynger and clawes þer to, Of peper and wyn þou take also, And salt hit þen and sethe hit wele. Cast in þy flesshe, hewen yche a dele, And messe hit forthe, as I þe kenne, Set hit in sale before goode menne. [Liber cure cocorum (England, 1430)]

6. Amydone

Recipes for amidon (wheat starch) aren't uncommon, and the ones found in Liber cure cocorum and A Noble Boke off Cookry are reasonably close to the Crophill version. However, both of those have notable differences. The recipe in Liber doesn't call for the water to be changed twice daily, and the one in Noble calls for steeping the wheat for ten days instead of nine.

> Amydone. Take wete and stepe hit dayes ix. Þus chaunge þy water yche day be dene. Brys hit in a morter ry3t smalle, Sethe

hit with mylke and water with alle. Þorowgh a herseve loke þou
hit sye, And let hit stonde and setel bye. Poure oute þe water,
in clothe hit lay, Tyl hit be drye þou turne hit ay. Þys is a lycour
as men sayn, Þer of I schalle speke more in playn. [Liber cure
cocorum (England, 1430)]

To mak amydon take whet and step it in water x dais and
change the water eury daye then bet yt smalle in a mortair and
sethe it with water and mylk and sye it throughe a clothe and
let yt stond and setelle and pour out the water and lay it in a
clothe and turn it till it be drye. [A Noble Boke off Cookry
(England, 1468)]

Interestingly, the version found in MS Harley 5401 is closest to the
Crophill recipe.

To make Amydon. Recipe whete & stepe it ix dayes, & change
þe water every day twyes; than bray it in a morter right small, &
clens it throgh a haryn syve, & lat it stonde tyll it be sett; þen
put onto þe morter & bray it in a clothe to it be dry. [MS
Harley 5401 (England, 15th century)]

7. Conyes in Grave
This is one of the more common recipes, with almost every
contemporary source having one or two different versions. As with
other recipes in Crophill, the versions from Liber and Noble are
particularly close. Others, such as the one from Forme of Cury,
tend to add sugar and leave out the wine.

Conyngus in gravé. Sethe welle þy conyngus in water clere,
After, in water colde þou wasshe hom sere, Take mylke of
almondes, lay hit anone With myed bred or amydone. Fors hit
with cloves or gode gyngere. Boyle hit over þo fyre, Hew þo
conyngus, do hom þer to, Seson hit with wyn or sugur þo.
[Liber cure cocorum (England, 1430)]

To mak conys in graue fley your conys and wesshe them and
sethe them then take almond mylk and alay it with bred or whit
amydon and fors it with clowes and galingale and boile yt welle

and hew your conys and boile yt welle and hew your ceripe and put them ther to and sesson it with wyne and sugur and serue it. [A Noble Boke off Cookry (England, 1468)]

Connynges In Grauey. XXVI. Take Connynges smyte hem to pecys. parboile hem and drawe hem with a gode broth with almandes blanched and brayed. do þerinne sugur and powdour gynger and boyle it and the flessh þerwith. flour it with sugur and with powdour gynger an serue forth. [Forme of Cury (England, 1390)]

8. Chikens in Cryteyne

This recipe is part of a broad family of recipes that go by a wide range of similar names, such as "cretonne", "cruton", "gretney", and "kirtin". The sauce for the dish varies widely as well, most being thickened with almond milk but some use eggs or flour instead. Again, the closest match for the *Crophill* version comes from *Liber* and *Noble*.

Chekyns in cretene. Take cow mylke, lye hit anone With flowre, or ellis with amydone. Fors hit with galyngale and gode gyngere, With canel and comyn, alle in fere, Coloure hit with safron þo. Þe chekyns by hom selfe þo sethe þer to, Hew hom in quarteres and lay hom inne, Boyle hom up with alle, no more ne mynne. But seson hit with sugur suete, And serve hom forthe for þay ben sete. [Liber cure cocorum (England, 1430)]

To dight chekins in kirtyne tak cow creme and alay it with flour or whit amydon and fors it with galingalle guinger canelle comyn and saffron then sethe your chekins and quarter them and sesson them with sugur and serue it. [A Noble Boke off Cookry (England, 1468)]

9. Viaunde de Cipre

This recipe also has a close match in Liber and Noble. There are recipes for Viand de Cypress in both Forme of Cury and MS Royal 12.C.xii as well, but those recipes are significantly different.

Viande de Cipur. Take braunne of capons or hennes þou shalle. Parboyle and drye hit with alle. Hew hom smalle, bray in mortere, As smalle as bred, þat myed were. Take good almonde mylke anone And lye hit up with amydone Or with floure of ryse, þou may. Coloure hit with safron, I þe say. Boyle hit after yche adele, Charge hit with flesshe brayed wele. Seson hit with sugur and þen þy dysshe With almondes set þou schalle florysshe. [Liber cure cocorum (England, 1430)]

To mak viand de cipre, tak the braun of capon or of henne parboille it and dry it then hew it smalle in a mortair and putt ther to almond mylk and lay it up with amydon or with flour of rise coloure it with saffron and boille it and chargant it with the braed braun and sesson it with sugur and florishe it with almondes and serue it. [A Noble Boke off Cookry (England, 1468)]

10. Maretrel de le Char
This recipe continues the sequence of recipes with clear matches in *Liber Cure Cocorum*.

Mortrews de chare. Take hennes and fresshe porke, y þe kenne, Sethe hom togedur alwayes þenne. Take hem up, pyke out þe bonys, Enbande þe porke, Syr, for þo nonys. Hew hit smalle and grynde hit wele, Cast it agayne, so have þou cele, In to þe brothe, and charge hit þenne With myed wastelle, as I þe kenne. Colour hit with safron, at þat tyde. Boyle hit and set hit doune be syde. Lye hit with ȝolkes of eren ryȝt, And florysshe þy dysshe with pouder þou myȝt. [Liber cure cocorum (England, 1430)]

There are also corresponding recipes in both *Forme of Cury* and *A Noble Boke off Cookry*.

Mortrews. XX.II. V. Take hennes and Pork and seeþ hem togyder. take the lyre of Hennes and of the Pork, and hewe it small and grinde it all to doust. take brede ygrated and do þerto, and temper it with the self broth and alye it with zolkes

23

of ayrenn, and cast þeron powdour fort, boile it and do þerin powdour of gyngur sugur. safroun and salt. and loke þer it be stondyng, and flour it with powdour gynger. [Forme of Cury (England, 1390)]

A Martins Of Flesche. Tak mortyns of flesche tak hennes and freche pork and sethe them to gedour then tak them up and enbane them for the nonse and hewe the pork and grain it and cast it in again and chargejour it with myed bred and colour it with saffron and boile it and set it down alay it with yolks of eggs and staunch it with pouder and serue it. [A Noble Boke off Cookry (England, 1468)]

11. Chaudone Potage of Pygys

There are versions of this recipe in both *Liber* and *Noble*, though they're closer to each other than they are to the *Crophill* verison. The change in the main ingredient and the spicing are especially interesting.

Þandon for wylde digges, swannus, and piggus. Take, wasshe þo isues of swannes anon, And skoure þo guttus with salt ichon. Sethe alle to gedur and hew hit smalle. Þe flesshe and eke þo guttus with alle. Take galingale and gode gyngere And canel, and grynd hom al in fere. And myude bred þou take þerto, And temper hit up with brothe also. Coloure hit with brend bred or with blode, Seson hit with venegur, a lytelle for gode. Welle alle togedur in a posnet. In service forthe þou schalt hit sett. [Liber cure cocorum [Sloane MS 1986] (England, 1430)]

To mak chaudron for swan wild duck or pigge take and wesshe the issus of a swan and skour the guttes with salt and sethe them to gedour and hewe small bothe the flesshes and the guttes and put ther to canelle or galingale put myed bred ther to and temper it with the brothe or with the blod and sesson it to venygar and boille them in a possuet and serue them furthe. [A Noble Boke off Cookry (England, 1468)]

12. Browes de Chaudoun

While there are plenty of surviving recipes for funnel cakes, I could not find anything for making fried dough balls like this recipe. The phrase "oyle de oyle" is most likely a copyist error for "oil de olive".

13. Noumbles of Net

Recipes for "numbles" are reasonably common in contemporary cookbooks. That being said, the corresponding recipes from *Liber* and *Noble* are particulary close matches to the *Crophill* version in that all three call for the heart, midriff, and kidney. None of the other sources specify those parts.

> Nombuls. Take þo hert and þo mydruv and þe kydnere, And hew hom smalle, as I þe lere. Presse oute þe blode, wasshe hom þou schalle, Sethe hom in water and in gode ale. Coloure hit with brende bred or with blode. Fors hit with peper and canel gode, Sett hit to þo fyre, as I þe telle in tale. Kele hit with a litelle ale, And set hit downe to serve in sale. [Liber cure cocorum (England, 1430)]

> To mak nombles tak hert middrif and kidney and hew them smalle and prise out the blod and sethe them in water and ale and colour it with brown bred or with blod and fors it with canell and galingalle and when it boilithe kole it a litille with ale and serwe it. [A Noble Boke off Cookry (England, 1468)]

On a side note, most of the recipes for numbles either specifically call for deer kidneys or do not specify the animal at all. In the *Crophill* version the title makes it clear that the organs should be from a neat (e.g. bull, cow, calf). This is further emphasized in the manuscript by the drawing of a bovine in the margin.

14. Roo in Sewe

Along with the two clearly related recipes from *Liber* and *Noble*, there is also one in *Ancient Cookery*.

Roo in a Sewe. Take þo roo, pyke hit clene forthy; Boyle hit þou shalt and after hit drye. Hew hit on gobettis, þat ben smalle, Do hit in pot withalle. Kest wyn þerto, if þou do ry3t, Take persole and sawge and ysope bry3t, Wasshe hom and hew hom wondur smalle, And do þerto hit þou schalle, Coloure hit with blode or sawnders hors. [Liber cure cocorum (England, 1430)]

Roo for Sewe. To mak roo in sewe tak the roo and pik it and boille it then hew it in gobettes and put it in the pot cast ther to wyne parsly saige and ysope and put them in the pot do ther to pepper guinger clowes saunders and blod and serue it. [A Noble Boke off Cookry (England, 1468)]

Roo in sene. Take flesh of a roo and pyke hit clene and parboyle hit, and then take hit up and drye hit wyth a clothe, and hewe hit on gobettes, and put it in a pot; and do thereto wyne and let it sethe, and take sage, parsel, ysope, and hewe hit smal, and put thereto pouder of pepur, and of clowes, and of canel, and colour it with blode, and let hit boyle, and serve hit forthe. [Ancient Cookery (England, 1425)]

What I find most interesting about these recipes is that they are much more similar to each other than they are to the *Crophill* version.

15. Counsis

While medieval recipes for stewed chicken are fairly common, the name of this one and the particular combination of ingredients is not. As with the previous recipe, there are corresponding versions in *Liber* and *Noble*. However, the third match for this one comes from *Forme of Cury* instead.

Capons in Covisye. Take capons and sethe hom wele, And hew hom smalle ilkadele. Take peper and brede, and grynde hit smalle, And temper hit up with capon alle. Take why3te of eyren harde soþun þo, And hake hom smalle and do þerto, And boyle þe capon and coloure hit þenne With safrone, and do as I kenne. Þo ȝolkes of eggus, I telle þe, Alle hole þou put in disshe so fre. [Liber cure cocorum (England, 1430)]

capon In Couns. To mak capons in couns tak a capon and sethe it and hew it then grind pepper and bred and temper it with the capon then tak the whit of egg herd sodene and hew them small and boile the capons and colour it with saffron and lay yolks of eggs in the disshe hole and serue it. [A Noble Boke off Cookry (England, 1468)]

VI - Caponys In Coneys. Schal be sodyn. Nym the lyre and brek it smal In a morter and peper and wyte bred therwyth and temper it wyth ale and ley it wyth the capoun. Nym hard sodyn eyryn and hewe the wyte smal and kaste thereto and nym the zolkys al hole and do hem in a dysch and boyle the capoun and colowre it wyth safroun and salt it and messe it forthe. [Forme of Cury (England, 1390)]

Again, the other versions seem to be more closely related to each other than to the *Crophill* version, with one notable difference being that the *Crophill* recipe calls for the capon to be roasted where all the other recipes have it boiled.

16. Let Lorres des Aguellys
This curious recipe for eel stew appears to be unique to Crophill. I could not find any similar recipes in contemporary sources, including those from outside of England.

17. Cherise
While there are no recipes for Cherise in *Liber* or *Noble*, there are two different versions in *Forme of Cury* and one in *Two Fifteenth-Century Cookery-Books*.

XVIII - FOR TO MAKE CHIRESEYE. Tak Chiryes at the Fest of Seynt John the Baptist and do away the stonys grynd hem in a morter and after frot hem wel in a seve so that the Jus be wel comyng owt and do than in a pot and do ther'in feyr gres or Boter and bred of wastrel ymyid and of sugur a god party and a porcioun of wyn and wan it is wel ysodyn and ydressyd in Dyschis stik ther'in clowis of Gilofr' and strew ther'on sugur. [Forme of Cury (England, 1390)]

Chyryse XX.II. XVIII. Take Almandes unblanched, waisshe hem, grynde hem, drawe hem up with gode broth. do þerto thridde part of chiryse. þe stones. take oute and grynde hem smale, make a layour of gode brede an powdour and salt and do þerto. colour it with sandres so that it may be stondyng, and florish it with aneys and with cheweryes, and strawe þeruppon and serue it forth. [Forme of Cury (England, 1390)]

Cxxiiij - Chyryoun. Take Chyryis, and pike out the stonys, waysshe hem clene in wyne, than wryng hem thorw a clothe, and do it on a potte, and do ther-to whyte grece a quantyte, and a partye of Floure of Rys, and make it chargeaunt; do ther-to hwyte Hony or Sugre, poynte it with Venegre; A-force it with stronge pouder of Canelle and of Galyngale, and a-lye it with a grete porcyoun of ʒolkys of Eyroun; coloure it with Safroun or Saunderys; and whan thou seruyste in, plante it with Chyrioun, and serue forth. [Two Fifteenth-Century Cookery-Books (England, 1430)]

The degree of variation in the recipes shows that there were a number of ways to make this dish, and also suggests that there was no strongly preferred method.

18. Soppes Dorre

While recipes for Soppes Dorry ("golden sops") are pretty common, it is interesting that this recipe is closer to the versions in *Forme of Cury* and *Two Fifteenth-Century Cookery-Books* than it is to the expected recipes in *Liber* and *Noble*.

Sowpus dorre. Take almondes, bray hem, wryng hom up. Boyle hom with wyn rede to sup. Þen temper hom with wyn, salt, I rede, And loke þou tost fyne wete brede, And lay in dysshes, dubene with wyne. Do in þis dysshes mete, þat is so fyne. Messe hit forthe, and florysshe hit þenne With sugur and gynger, as I þe kenne. [Liber cure cocorum (England, 1430)]

To mak soupes dorrey tak almondes and bray them asid wring them up and boile them with wyn and temper them with wyne and salt then toost whit bred and lay it in a disshe and enbane it with wyne and pour it ouer the met and florisshe it with sugur and guingere and serue it. [A Noble Boke off Cookry (England, 1468)]

VI - FOR TO MAKE SOWPYS DORRY. Nym onyons and mynce hem smale and fry hem in oyl dolyf Nym wyn and boyle yt wyth the onyouns roste wyte bred and do yt in dischis and god Almande mylk also and do ther'above and serve yt forthe. [Forme of Cury (England, 1390)]

Soupes dorrees. Nym oynons, mynce hem, frie hem in oille de olyue: nym oynons, boille hem with wyn, tost whit bred, and do it in dishes / and cast almand mylke theron, and ye wyn and ye oynons aboue, and gif hit forth. [Two Fifteenth-Century Cookery-Books (England, 1430)]

One curious note, the *Crophill* version of the recipe appears to be the only one that suggests using ale instead of wine.

19. Blawmanger of Lekys
This recipe is a bit of an oddity. In spite of its name, it doesn't resemble the blancmanger (rice and chicken) recipes commonly found in other sources. However it does seem to be related to several recipes titled "blanch porry".

For blaunchyd porray. Take thykke mylke of almondes dere And heke hedes þou take with stalk in fere, Þat is in peses þou stryke. Put alle in pot, alye hit ilyke With a lytel floure, and serve hit þenne Wele soþun, in sale, before gode menne. [Liber cure cocorum (England, 1430)]

xlv - For to make Blawnche Perrye. Take the Whyte of the lekys, an sethe hem in a potte, an presse hem vp, and hacke hem smal on a bord. An nym gode Almaunde Mylke, an a lytil of Rys, an do alle thes to-gederys, an sethe an stere it wyl, an

do ther-to Sugre or hony, an dresse it yn; thanne take powderd
Elys, an sethe hem in fayre Water, and broyle hem, an kytte
hem in long pecys. And ley .ij. or .iij. in a dysshe, and putte thin
perrey in a-nother dysshe, an serue the to dysshys to-gederys as
Venysoun with Furmenty. [Two Fifteenth-Century Cookery-
Books (England, 1430)]

Blanche porrey. Take blanche almondes, And grinde hem, and
drawe hem with sugur water thorgh a streynour into a good
stuff mylke into a potte; and then take the white of lekes, and
hew hem small, and grynde hem in a morter with brede; and
then cast al to the mylke into the potte, and caste therto sugur
and salt, and lete boyle; And seth feyre poudrid eles in faire
water ynowe, and broile hem on a gredren; and kut hem in
faire longe peces, and ley two or thre in a dissh togidre as ye do
veneson with ffurmenty, And serue it forthe. [Two Fifteenth-
Century Cookery-Books (England, 1430)]

Blaunche pore. Take thyke melke of almondys do yt in a potte
perboyle the whyte of lekys tendour presse out the watyre hew
hem smalle grynd hem temper hem with the same mylke do to
gedyr with sygure and salt boyle hit up yf thu wilte thu
mayste alay with payndemayn othir with cromys of white brede
draw hem with the same mylke and serve hit forth with salte
ele yf thu have hit. [Recipes from the Wagstaff Miscellany
(England, 1460)]

20. Browet of Almayne

There are versions of this recipe in both *Liber* and *Noble*, and again
those recipes are closer to each other than to the *Crophill* version.

Breuet de almonde. Take gode almonde mylke anon, And loke
þou lye hit with amydone, Or with flowre þat is bake. Coloure
hit with safron, I undurtake. Fors hit with powder of þy male
Of gyngere, canel, and galingale. Take pertrykes and chykyns
and hom wele sethe. Hew hom in quarters fayre and smethe.
Do þat mylke over þo fyre þat tyde, And boyle and sett hit
doune besyde, And florysshe hit with powdur, as I þe kenne,

Þou may have more menske emong alle menne. [Liber cure cocorum (England, 1430)]

To mak Bruet de almondes tak almond mylk and alay it with amydon or with whet flour bulted coloure it with saffron and fors it with pouder of ginger canelle and galingale then tak pertuche or chekens and sethe them and hew them in quarto and set the mylk on the fyere to boylle and florish it with pouders and serue it [A Noble Boke off Cookry (England, 1468)]

In this particular case, the differences may not be as strange as they first seem. The versions of the recipe from other sources show that there is a great amount of variation in both ingredients and instructions for making "Brewet of Almonds".

Bruet of Almayn. Take beef or porke chopyd in pecys cast hem yn a pott grynd almondys draw hem with swete brothe & put hit yn the flesch boyle hit & put ther to poudyr of pepyr & sygure when hit ys yboyled y nowghe sesyn hit up with poudyr of gynger & vergeys & coloure hit al rede as blode with. [Recipes from the Wagstaff Miscellany (England, 1460)]

Browet of almayne. Take conynges and parboyle hom, and choppe hom on gobettus, and rybbes of porke or of kydde, and do hit in a pot, and fethe hit; then take almondes and grynde hom, and tempur hit up wyth broth of beef, and do hit in a pot; and take clowes, maces, pynes, ginger mynced, and rayfynges of corance; and take onyons and boyle hom, then cut hom and do hom in the pot; and colour hit with saffron, and let hit boyle; and take the flesh oute from the brothe and caste therto; and take alkenet and frye hit, and do hit in the pot thurgh a streynour; and in the fettynge doun put therto a lytel vynegar, and pouder of gynger medelet togedur, and serve hit forth. [Ancient Cookery (England, 1425)]

Brewet Of Almony. XX.II. VII. Take Conynges or kiddes and hewe hem small on moscels oþer on pecys. parboile hem with the same broth, drawe an almaunde mylke and do the fleissh þerwith, cast þerto powdour galyngale & of gynger with flour

31

of Rys. and colour it wiþ alkenet. boile it, salt it. & messe it forth with sugur and powdour douce. [Forme of Cury (England, 1390)]

Bruet of Almaynne. Take Almaundys, and draw a gode mylke ther-of with Water; take Capoun, Conyngys or Pertriches; smyte the Capoun, or kede, or Chykonys, Conyngys: the Pertriche shal ben hol: than blaunche the Fleyssh, an caste on the mylke; take larde and mynce it, and caste ther-to; take an mynce Oynonys and caste ther-to y-nowe, do Clowes and smal Roysonys ther-to; caste hol Safroun ther-to, than do it to the fyre, and stere it wyl; whan the fleysshe ys y-now, sette it on the fyre, an do ther-to Sugre y-now; take pouder Gyngere, Galyngale, Canel, and temper the pouder wyth Vynegre, .& caste ther-to; sesyn it with salt, and serue forth. [Two Fifteenth-Century Cookery-Books (England, 1430)]

Browet d'Alemaigne. Take almond milk, sifted cloves of gillyflowers, cubebs, fried onions; and it must be hot with cloves and cubebs; color, yellow. [MS Royal 12.C.xii (England/France, 1340)]

21. Rys Rayle
I could not find any other version of this recipe, though there are recipes in *Liber* and *Noble* titled "Mortrews" that are similar.

For blanchyd mortrews. Sethe hennes and porke, þat is fulle fresshe. Bray almondes unblanchyd and temper hom nesshe With clene brothe, and drawe hom þo. Alay þy flesshe smalle grounden to, And floure of ryce þou grynd also. Cast powder of gyngere and sugur þerinne, But loke þat hit be not to þyn, But stondand and saltid mesurlé And kepe þy dysshe mete for þo maystré. [Liber cure cocorum (England, 1430)]

Mortrews. XX.II. V. Take hennes and Pork and seeþ hem togyder. take the lyre of Hennes and of the Pork, and hewe it small and grinde it all to doust. take brede ygrated and do þerto, and temper it with the self broth and alye it with zolkes of ayrenn, and cast þeron powdour fort, boile it and do þerin powdour of gyngur sugur. safroun and salt. and loke þer it be stondyng, and flour it with powdour gynger. [Forme of Cury (England, 1390)]

Given that the word "rice" shows up in the title of the recipe but doesn't appear in the recipe itself, this might be a case where the copyist unintentionally merged two different recipes.

22. Pochee

There are a handful of recipes with titles related to "pochee", but all of them other than the *Crophill* version are centered around eggs (e.g. "poached").

Pochee. XX.IIII. X. Take Ayrenn and breke hem in scaldyng hoot water. and whan þei bene sode ynowh. take hem up and take zolkes of ayren and rawe mylke and swyng hem togydre, and do þerto powdour gyngur safroun and salt, set it ouere the fire, and lat it not boile, and take ayrenn isode & cast þe sew onoward. & serue it forth. [Forme of Cury(England, 1390)]

Eyron en poche. Take Eyroun, breke hem, an sethe hem in hot Water; than take hem Vppe as hole as thou may; than take flowre, an melle with Mylke, and caste ther-to Sugre or Hony, and a lytel pouder Gyngere, an boyle alle y-fere, and coloure with Safroun; an ley thin Eyroun in dysshys, and caste the Sewe a-boue, and caste on pouder y-now. Blawnche pouder ys best. [Two Fifteenth-Century Cookery-Books (England, 1430)]

The recipes that appear to be more closely related to *Crophill's* pochee are the "figey" recipes in Liber and Nobel.

To mak a figge tak figges and boile them in wyne then bray them in a mortair put ther to bred and boile it with wyne cast ther to clowes maces guinger pynes and hole, raissins and florisshe it withe pongarnettes and serue it. [A Noble Boke off Cookry (England, 1468)]

For stondand fygnade. Fyrst play þy water with hony and salt, Grynde blanchyd almondes I wot þou schalle. Þurghe a streynour þou shalt hom streyne, With þe same water þat is so clene. In sum of þe water stepe þou shalle Whyte brede crustes to alye hit with alle. Þenne take figgus and grynde hom wele, Put hom in pot so have þou cele. Þen take brede, with mylke hit streyne Of almondes þat be white and clene. Cast in þo fyggus þat ar igrynde With powder of peper þat is þo kynde, And powder of canel. in grete lordys house With sugur or hony þou may hit dowce. Þen take almondes cloven in twen, Þat fryid ar with oyle, and set with wyn Þy disshe, and florysshe hit þou my3t With powder of gyngere þat is so bry3t, And serve hit forthe as I spake thenne And set hit in sale before gode menne. [Liber cure cocorum (England, 1430)]

Two possible explanations come to mind for the *Crophill* version. The first is that the wrong title somehow got attached to the recipe. The second is that the recipe is for a meatless version of the more common pochee recipes.

23. Browet Mese
This confusingly-worded recipe appears to be unique. The closest matches given below have similar elements, but it is not clear if they're meant to be the same recipes.

Browet salmenee. Vinegar, galingale, cinnamon, powder of cloves of gillyflowers in great abundance; soft eggs, and sugar in great abundance to cut the strength of the spice; thick with the spice of ginger; color, black or green. [MS Royal 12.C.xii (England/France, 1340)]

Vyaund de cyprys bastarde. Take gode wyne, and Sugre next Aftyrward, and caste to-gedere; thenne take whyte Gyngere, and Galyngale, and Canel fayre y-mynced; then take Iuse of Percile and Flowre of Rys, and Brawn of Capoun and of Chykonnys I-grounde, and caste ther-to; An coloure it wyth Safroun and Saunderys, an a-ly it with 3olkys of Eyroun, and make it chargeaunt; an whan thou dressest it yn, take Maces,

Clowes, Quybibes, and straw a-boue, and serue forth. [Two Fifteenth-Century Cookery-Books (England, 1430)]

24. Crane

In spite of the title of this recipe, it doesn't appear to have anything to do with cranes, nor does it even remotely resemble crane recipes from other sources. The title could be a copyist error for "cream" though, and there are other recipes for "cream of almond milk" that appear at least vaguely related.

> Crem of almonde mylk. Take almonde mylke, and boyle hit, and when hit is boylet take hit from the fyre, and springe theron a lytel vynegur; then take and cast hit on a clothe, and cast theron sugur, and when hit is colde gedur hit together, and leche hit in dysshes, and serve hit forthe. [Ancient Cookery (England, 1425)]

> Creme Of Almaundes. XX.IIII. V. Take Almaundes blaunched, grynde hem and drawe hem up thykke, set hem ouer the fyre & boile hem. set hem adoun and spryng hem wicii Vyneger, cast hem abrode uppon a cloth and cast uppon hem sugur. whan it is colde gadre it togydre and leshe it in dysshes. [Forme of Cury (England, 1390)]

Another possibility is that the recipe is mistitled, as it appears similar to the following from *Liber* and *Noble*.

> Caudel dalmone. Take almondes unblanchyd and hom þou bray. Drawe hom up with wyn, I dar wele say. Þer to do pouder of good gyngere And sugur, and boyle alle þese in fere, And coloure hit with safron and salt hit wele, And serve hit forthe Sir at þo mele. [Liber cure cocorum (England, 1430)]

> To mak cawdelle dalmond tak unblanched almondes and bray them and draw them with wyne put ther to pouder of guinger and sugur and boile all to gedur and colore it with saffron and salt it and serue it. [A Noble Boke off Cookry (England, 1468)]

25. Charlet Gentyl

While there are many reciped for charlete in other sources, none of them are a very close match for the *Crophill* version and none are "gentyl". The charlet recipes from *Liber* and *Noble* are good examples.

> Charlet. Take swettest mylke, þat þou may have, Colour hit with safron, so God þe save. Take fresshe porke and sethe hit wele, And hew hit smalle every dele. Swyng eyryn, and do þer to. Set hit over þe fyre, þenne Boyle hit and sture lest hit brenne. Whenne hit welles up, þou schalt hit kele With a litel ale, so have þou cele. When hit is inoʒe, þou sett hit doune, And kepe hit lest hit be to broune.   Liber cure cocorum (England, 1430)]

> To mak charlet tak swet mylk and colour it with saffron then tak freche pork and boile it and hew yt smalle then swinge eggs and cast them into the mylk and boile them and stirr them lest they bren and bete it with a litill ale and set it doun and let it not be brown and serue it.   [A Noble Boke off Cookry (England, 1468)]

Interestingly, there is a non-charlet recipe from *Two Fifteenth-Century Cookery-Books* with the word "gentyl" in the name which may be related.

> Crustade gentyle. Take a Cofyn y-bake; than grynd Porke or Vele smal with harde ʒolkys of Eyroun; than lye it with Almaunde Milke, and make hem stondyng; take Marow of bonys, and ley on the cofynne, and fylle hem fulle with thin comade, and serue forth.   [Two Fifteenth-Century Cookery-Books (England, 1430)]

26. Viaunde de Cipre

Viand Cypress is one of the more common medieval recipes and there are versions in almost every surviving cookbook from that period. The versions from *Liber* and *Noble*, while not an exact match, are reasonalbly close to the *Crophill* verison.

Viande de Cipur. Take braunne of capons or hennes þou shalle. Parboyle and drye hit with alle. Hew hom smalle, bray in mortere, As smalle as bred, þat myed were. Take good almonde mylke anone And lye hit up with amydone Or with floure of ryse, þou may. Coloure hit with safron, I þe say. Boyle hit after yche adele, Charge hit with flesshe brayed wele. Seson hit with sugur and þen þy dysshe With almondes set þou schalle florysshe. [Liber cure cocorum (England, 1430)]

To mak viand de cipre, tak the braun of capon or of henne parboille it and dry it then hew it smalle in a mortair and putt ther to almond mylk and lay it up with amydon or with flour of rise coloure it with saffron and boille it and chargant it with the braed braun and sesson it with sugur and florishe it with almondes and serue it. [A Noble Boke off Cookry (England, 1468)]

27. Viaunde de Burgeoun
This is another recipe that seems a bit cryptic. There is a recipe in *Ancient Cookery* with a similar title that seems to be related, but the text of the recipe is very different.

Viande Burton for xl mees. Take vlb. of dates, ii lb. of reyfynges of sypres, and fethe hom all in red wync; and then bray hom with vernage, with a fewe chippes of light bred stepet in vernage, with clowes and canell; and when hit is brayed drawe up al togedur thik thurgh a streynour, and put hit in a clene pot, and boyle hit, and in the boylinge take iilb. of sugre, and travaile hit wel; and take the zolkes of eyren, and a quartron of gynger mynced, and caste the gynger in the fame pot, and travaile hit wel, and take the zolkes beforefayde, and bete hom wel togeder, and streyne hom thurgh a streynour; and in the scttynge downe of the pot, bete in the eyren, and bete in ther among di. a quartron of pouder of gynger, and put in a few faunders, and saffron, ande salt, and water of euerose; and if hit be for a lorde, put vii leches in a difshe, or v, and make a dragge of syne sugre, and triet pouder of ginger, and of

anys in confit, and strawe hit theron; and serve hit forthe.
[Ancient Cookery (England, 1425)]

There is a recipe from *Wagstaff* that could be a version of Viand
Burton, but again there are significant differences. All three of
these could be related, or they could just be part of a larger
category of recipes that have some similar aspects.

> Viaund ryall. Grynd reysons draw with bastard clare osey or
> othir swete wyn the best thu may gete take datys cut grete
> reysons of coraunce clovis macys pynes & floure of canel yf
> thu have hit pure hit in a pot & som of the good wyn ther with
> when hit ys boyled y nowghe take the syrip of the resons & the
> creme of almonds & past ryall & pynad and gobet ryal &
> gynger in confite & claryfyd quynsys or chard wardys poudyr
> poudyr of canell do al thes to gedyr yn a pot set hit on the fyre
> stere hit wel when hit ys at the boylyng take hit of loke hit be
> doucet and that hit have y nowgh of poudres & somdell of salt
> deresse hit forth as a flate potage & yf thu serve hit forth
> colour hit with blossemys of safron have fisch braune sodyn
> tendyr & draw yn thorowgh a streynour & colour hit with
> safron that hit be as brythe as lambur when hit ys cold floresch
> the sewe ther with in dysches & serve hit forthe. [Recipes
> from the Wagstaff Miscellany (England, 1460)]

28. Burgeoun de Vyne
Aside from being somewhat cryptic, this recipe also appears to be
unique. I could not find any comparable recipes in other sources.

29. Rys Camelyn
I could not find any other versions of this recipe. While there are a
number of vaguely similar recipes in other sources, the similarities
might only be due to the *Crophill* recipe consisting of very common
ingredients.

30. A Stywe
This simple recipe does not seem to have any close matches in

other sources. It is similar to the "Stewed Lombard" recipe from Noble, except that it lacks both onions and almonds. Similarly, it has a lot in common with galantine recipes such as the one from Liber, but does not include the bread crusts that is the first ingredient in all of those recipes.

To mak stewed lombard tak pork and rost it and chop it into a pot with wyne sugur and hole clowes onyons guingere saffron and sanders then fry almondes and temper them up with wyne pouder gyngyure canelle and galingale and serue it. [A Noble Boke off Cookry (England, 1468)]

Galentyne. Take crust of brede and grynde hit smalle, Take powder of galingale and temper with alle Powder of gyngere and salt also. Temper hit with venegur er þou more do, Draw3e hit þurughe a streynour þenne, And messe hit forthe before gode menne. [Liber cure cocorum (England, 1430)]

31. A Gelle
Recipes for jelly (gelatin) are very common, but also vary widely. The version from *Noble* is notably different from the *Crophill* recipe.

To mak a gilly of fleshe take conys and fley them and skald pegions chop them and fley of the skyne skald chekins and chope kiddes and put all to gedur and boile it in red wyne then tak it upe and lay it in a clene clothe dry the peces of the kid pigions and conys and couche them in dishe and chope chekkins and put ther to then set the chekkins in a cold place where it may stand stille then set the brothe to the fyere agayne and luk it be well strened that no fat abid ther on then tak skalded caluys feet and lay them in the same brothe till they be tender and luk the brothe be clene scomed sessen it up with salt and serue it. [A Noble Boke off Cookry (England, 1468)]

32. Garbage
The *Crophill* recipe for "garbage" is unusual in that all of the other recipes by that name specify that the main ingredient is offal from poultry.

To mak a garbage tak the heed the garbage the leuer the gessern the wings and the feet and wesche them and clene them and put them in a pot and cast ther to brothe of beef poudere of pepper clowes maces parsly saige mynced then step bred in the sam brothe and cast it to pouder of guingere venygar saffron and salt and serue it. [A Noble Boke off Cookry (England, 1468)]

Garbage. Take fayre garbagys of chykonys, as the hed, the fete, the lyuerys, an the gysowrys; washe hem clene, an caste hem in a fayre potte, an caste ther-to freysshe brothe of Beef or ellys of moton, an let it boyle; an a-lye it wyth brede, an ley on Pepir an Safroun, Maces, Clowys, an a lytil verious an salt, an serue forth in the maner as a Sewe. [Two Fifteenth-Century Cookery-Books (England, 1430)]

Garbage. Take faire Garbage, chikenes hedes, ffete, lyvers, And gysers, and wassh hem clene; caste hem into a faire potte, And caste fressh broth of Beef, powder of Peper, Canell, Clowes, Maces, Parcely and Sauge myced small; then take brede, stepe hit in the same brothe, Drawe hit thorgh a streynour, cast thereto, And lete boyle ynowe; caste there-to pouder ginger, vergeous, salt, And a litull Safferon, And serve hit forthe. [Two Fifteenth-Century Cookery-Books (England, 1430)]

It could be that the flesh called for in the *Crophill* version is intended to be offal, but given how little it has in common with the other recipes, it is just as likely that the recipe is mistitled.

33. Counses

This recipe is a clear match with the recipes for "capons in councys" found in other sources, including *Liber* and *Noble*.

Capons in Covisye. Take capons and sethe hom wele, And hew hom smalle ilkadele. Take peper and brede, and grynde hit smalle, And temper hit up with capon alle. Take whyȝte of eyren harde soþun þo, And hake hom smalle and do þerto, And boyle þe capon and coloure hit þenne With safrone, and do as I kenne. Þo ȝolkes of eggus, I telle þe, Alle hole þou put in disshe so fre. [Liber cure cocorum (England, 1430)]

To mak capons in couns tak a capon and sethe it and hew it then grind pepper and bred and temper it with the capon then tak the whit of egg herd sodene and hew them small and boile the capons and colour it with saffron and lay yolks of eggs in the disshe hole and serue it. [A Noble Boke off Cookry (England, 1468)]

Capouns In Councys. XXII. Take Capons and rost hem right hoot þat þey be not half y nouhz and hewe hem to gobettes and cast hem in a pot, do þerto clene broth, seeþ hem þat þey be tendre. take brede and þe self broth and drawe it up yferer, take strong Powdour and Safroun and Salt and cast þer to. take ayrenn and seeþ hem harde. take out the zolkes and hewe the whyte þerinne, take the Pot fro þe fyre and cast the whyte þerinne. messe the disshes þerwith and lay the zolkes hool and flour it with clowes. [Forme of Cury (England, 1390)]

There is also a recipe in *Wagstaff* that is clearly related to the above.

Capons yne conceps. Take capons halfe rostyde do hem yn a pott put ther to swete broth & a perty of rede wyne stew hit up to gedyr that hit be ynowghe trye the brothe yf thu wylte thu may do ther to a lytyll lyoure of payndemayn take eyron sodyn harde hew the white do ther to sigure safron & salt set hit on the fyre when hit boyles a lay hit up withe yolkes of eyron loke hit be rennyng sesyn hit up withe poudyr of gynger & vergeys a rese the thyys & the whyngez & the brestz of the capons loke that they honge by ley hem yn disches plante hem withe hard yolkes of eyron and poudyr & the sewe a bovyn. [Recipes from the Wagstaff Miscellany (England, 1460)]

34. Cyvee

While civey recipes—meat with onions in gravy—are fairly common, they usually call for coney or hare. The closest recipes from *Liber* and *Noble* are good examples.

Conyngus in cyne. Smyte þe conyngus in pese smalle. And sethe hom in brothe gode þou shalle. Mynsyn onyons in grece þou sethe, And in good brothe, þat is so smethe Walle togeder. and drauȝe alioure Of blode and brede sumdele sowre, Sesonut with venegur and good brothe eke, Kast salt þerto and powder fulle meke. [Liber cure cocorum (England, 1430)]

To mak conys in cevy smyt conys in small peces and sethe them in good brothe put ther to mynced onyons and grece and draw a liour of broun bred and blod and sesson it with venygar and cast on pouder and salt and serve it. [A Noble Boke off Cookry (England, 1468)]

It could be that the *Crophill* version's use of capon is a copyist error. Then again, the original author may simply have preferred capon over coney.

35. Rosee
Roses were often used in medieval cooking, and there corresponding recipes called "rosee" in both *Liber* and *Noble*.

Rose. Take flour of ryse, as whyte as sylke, And hit welle, with almond mylke. Boyle hit tyl hit be chargyd, þenne Take braune of capone or elle of henne. Loke þou grynd hit wondur smalle, And sithen þou charge hit with alle. Coloure with alkenet, sawnder, or ellys with blode, Fors hit with clowes or macys gode. Seson hit with sugur grete plenté, Þis is a rose, as kokes telle me. [Liber cure cocorum (England, 1430)]

To mak rose, tak flour of ryse and temper it with almond mylk and mak it chaungynge then tak the braun of capon or of henne sodyn and grind it and charge it ther with and colour it with sanders and blod and fors it with clowes and maces and sesson it with sugur and serue it. [A Noble Boke off Cookry (England, 1468)]

36. Prymerose
While there is no recipe for primrose in *Liber*, there one in *Noble*.

There is also a version of the recipe in *Two Fifteenth-Century Cookery-Books*.

> To mak prymerolle in pasthe tak blanched almondes and flour of prymerose grind it and temper it with swet wyne and good brothe drawinge into the thik mylk put it into a pot with sugur salt and saffron that it haue colour lik prymerolle and boile it that it be stondinge and alay it with flour of rise and serue it as a standinge potage and strawe ther on flour of prymerolle aboue and ye may diaper it with rape rialle in dressinge of some other sewe. [A Noble Boke off Cookry (England, 1468)]

> Prymerose. Take other half-pound of Flowre of Rys, .iiij. pound of Almaundys, half an vnce of hony and Safroune, and take the flowres of the Prymerose, and grynd hem, and temper hem vppe with Mylke of the Almaundys, and do pouder Gyngere ther-on: boyle it, and plante thin skluce with Rosys, and serue forth [Two Fifteenth-Century Cookery-Books (England, 1430)]

37. Cewe de Kounsye

I could not find any other versions of this odd little recipe. The closest match is the following recipe from *Noble*, but there are significant differences (e.g. vinegar in the *Noble* recipe) that make me uncertain if they're truly related.

> To mak sauce aliper for rostid bef tak broun bred and stepe it in venygar and toiste it and streyne it and stampe garlik and put ther to pouder of pepper and salt and boile it a litill and serue it. [A Noble Boke off Cookry, (England, 1468)]

38. Farsure of Wych

I could not find any matches for this recipe in the other surviving cookbooks. From its brevity and confused wording, I expect that it is an incomplete and/or inaccurate copy from another source. I am also fairly sure that the word "wych" in the title is a copyist error for "fysch".

39. Tarts of Flesch

There are recipes in *Liber* and *Noble* that appear to be related to this recipe, but then there are many variations of meat pies in medieval cookbooks, so the common aspects could be a coincidence.

Tartlotes. Take porke sothun, and grynde hit wele With safroune, and medel hit ylkadel With egges and raysyns of corouns. þo Take powder and salt, and do þerto. Make a fole of doghe, and close þis fast, This flesshe þat hewene was open þo last Kover hit with lyddes, and pynche hit fayre, Korven in þe myddes two loyseyns a payr, Set hit with fryed almondes sere, And coloure þe past with safroune dere, And bake hit forthe, as I þe kenne, And set in sale before gode menne. [Liber cure cocorum (England, 1430)]

To mak tartes of fleshe tak pork and pik out the bones and grind it smale then boile figges in the freche brothe of flesche of wyne or of ale hewe it and grind it with egge then paire tender ches and grind ther with and let the most part stand by flesche then tak pynes and raissins and fry them a litille in grece and put it to the other with hole clowes maces poudur of pepper and cannele a goodele of guinger saffron sugur or hony clarified then salt it and toile them welle to gedur while the grece is hot, and mak gret coffynes with lowe liddes and ye may strawe ther to clowes maces and mynced dates whedur ye wille mold them with the stuf or strawe them aboue, and lay on the liddes wild werks and endor them with mylk of almondes and saffron and endore them as ye bak them and serue them furthe. [A Noble Boke off Cookry (England, 1468)]

Tartes of Flesch. Take porke sodyn pyke hit clene from thy bonys grynd hit small boyle fyggys in the broth of the flesch or yn wyn or in ale hew hit & grynd hit with eyron pare tendyr chese grynd hit to gedyr that the most perte stond by the flesch & the lest by the chese take pynes & reysons fry hem in a quantite of fresch grece & do hit in that othir with hole clowys macys & poudyr of pepyr & canell a grete dele & poudyr of gynger & sygure claryfyd or hony claryfyd safron & salt toyl hit well togedyr tyl thy grece be hote then make brode cofnys with

44

the brerdys as thyn as thu may make hem thu nay chese of clovys or mynsyd datys whethir thu wilte medyl hem with the stuff or els strew hem above & ley on the ledys close hem & thu may put ther yn lyghte worke & make endoryng with mylke of almondys & safron & endore hem or thu bake hem. [Recipes from the Wagstaff Miscellany (England, 1460)]

Interestingly, it's a recipe from *Forme of Cury* that comes closest to the *Crophill* version.

TARTES OF FLESH. XX.VIII. VIII. Take Pork ysode and grynde it smale. tarde harde eyrenn isode & ygrounde and do þerto with Chese ygronde. take gode powdour and hool spices, sugur, safroun, and salt & do þerto. make a coffyn as to feel sayde & do þis þerinne, & plaunt it with smale briddes istyned & counyng. & hewe hem to smale gobettes & bake it as tofore. & serue it forth. [Forme of Cury (England, 1390)]

40. Mawmene

Mawmany recipes are not uncommon, and there are versions in both *Liber* and *Noble* that are somewhat similar. It is worth noting that the *Crophill* recipe is unique in leaving out the wine.

For to make momene. Take whyte wyne, I telle þe, And sugur þerto ry3t grete plenté. Take, bray þo brawne of a3t capon. To a pot of oyle of on galon, And of hony a qwharte þou take. Do hit þer to as ever þou wake, Take powder þo mountenaunce of a pownde, And galingale ginger and canel rownde, And cast þer to, and styre hit. þenne Alle in on pot sethe hit, I kenne. [Liber cure cocorum (England, 1430)]

To mak mamony, tak whit wyne and sugur then bray the braun of viii capons with a gal on of oile and a quart of hony put ther to poudur of pepper galingalle guingere and canelle and stirre it welle and serue it. [A Noble Boke off Cookry (England, 1468)]

On a side note, the only mawmany recipe I found to specify the amount of sugar to be use is the following one from *Forme of Cury*, though the rest of the recipe is very unlike the *Crophill* verison.

Mawmenee. XX. Take a pottel of wyne greke. and ii. pounde of sugur take and clarifye the sugur with a qantite of wyne an drawe it thurgh a straynour in to a pot of erthe take flour of Canell. and medle with sum of the wyne an cast to gydre. take pynes with Dates and frye hem a litell in grece oþer in oyle and cast hem to gydre. take clowes an flour of canel hool and cast þerto. take powdour gyngur. canel. clower, colour it with saundres a lytel yf hit be nede cast salt þerto. and lat it seeþ; warly with a slowe fyre and not to thyk, take brawn of Capouns yteysed. oþer of Fesauntes teysed small and cast þerto. [Forme of Cury (England, 1390)]

41. Browet of Sarasynes

There are a variety of surviving recipes for "Brewet of Saracens," but none in *Liber* or *Noble*, and none of others are quite like the *Crophill* version.

FOR TO MAK A BRUET OF SARCYNESSE. Tak the lyre of the fresch Buf and bet it al in pecis and bred and fry yt in fresch gres tak it up and and drye it and do yt in a vessel wyth wyn and sugur and powdre of clowys boyle yt togedere tyl the flesch have drong the liycoure and take the almande mylk and quibibz macis and clowys and boyle hem togedere tak the flesch and do thereto and messe it forth. [Forme of Cury (England, 1390)]

Bruette Sareson. Take Almaundys and draw a gode mylke and flowre of Rys, and Porke and Brawen of Capoun y-sode, or Hennys smale y-grounde, and boyle it y-fere, and do in-to the mylke; and than take pouder Gyngere, Sugre, and caste a-boue, an serue forth. [Two Fifteenth-Century Cookery-Books (England, 1430)]

Bruet sarcenes. Take venyson boyle hit trye hit do hit yn a pott take almond mylke drawyn up with the same brothe cast ther yn onyons & a ley hit up withe floure of rye & caste yn cloves aftyr the boylyng take hit don sensyn hit up with poudyr wyn

& sygure & coloure hit with alekenet. [Recipes from the Wagstaff Miscellany (England, 1460)]

42. Browet Seche

There are recipes with similar names in *Two Fifteenth-Century Cookery-Books* and *MS Royal 12.C.xii*. Neither of them is very close to the *Crophill* recipe, but they each have some common aspects.

> Bruette saake. Take Capoun, skalde hem, draw hem, smyte hem to gobettys, Waysshe hem, do hem in a potte; thenne caste owt the potte, waysshe hem a-ȝen on the potte, and caste ther-to half wyne half Brothe; take Percely, Isope, Waysshe hem, and hew hem smal, and putte on the potte ther the Fleysshe is; caste ther-to Clowys, quybibes, Maces, Datys y-tallyd, hol Safroune; do it ouer the fyre; take Canelle, Gyngere, tempere thin powajes with wyne; caste in-to the potte Salt ther-to, hele it, and whan it is y-now, serue it forth. [Two Fifteenth-Century Cookery-Books (England, 1430)]

> Browet sek. Sweet broth, grape verjuice, ground parsley put therein, cloves, mace, cubebs; in times of chicks after Easter; and it will have the taste of good spices, saffron cooked therein with parsley in the broth; color, yellow. [MS Royal 12.C.xii (England/France, 1340)]

Interestingly, there is a recipe in *Liber* with a different name that is similar to the one from *Royal*, but it is hard to tell if it is intended to be the same recipe.

> Chekyns in browet. Take chekyns, scalde hom fayre and clene. Take persole, sauge, oþer herbȝ, grene Grapus, and stope þy chekyns with wynne. Take goode brothe, sethe hom þerinne, So þat þay sone boyled may be. Coloure þe brothe with safrone fre, And cast þeron powder dowce, For to be served in goode mennys howse. [Liber cure cocorum (England, 1430)]

43. Browet Ingse

I could not find any other versions of this recipe in medieval

English cookbooks. The recipe's name suggests "English Brewet," and while there are some medieval French recipes by that name, they don't seem to describe the same dish.

> For a subtle English brouet - If you want to make subtle English brouet, take hens and cook the livers, then take chestnuts then cut them from the hulls and grind together, then temper with the broth that the hens were cooked in, and add ginger, saffron and long pepper and mix with clear broth, then put together. [Enseignements (France, ca. 1300)]

> Subtle Broth from England. Take cooked peeled sweet chestnuts, and as many or more hard-boiled egg yolks and pork liver: grind all together, mix with warm water, then put through a sieve; then grind ginger, cinnamon, clove, grain, long pepper, galingale and saffron to give it color and set to boil together. [Le Menagier de Paris (France, 1393)]

44. Blaunch Desorre

Blanc de Syre is one of the more common recipes in medieval English cookbooks, so it's no surprise that there is a corresponding version in both *Liber* and *Noble*.

> Blonk desore. Take ryse and wasshe hom in a cup, Grynd hom smalle and temper up With almonde mylke, so have þou cele. Do hit over þo fyre and boyle hit wele. Take braune of capons or hennes alle, Hew hit þat hit be riȝt smalle. And grynd hit wele, as myud brede, And do þer to, as I þe rede. Seson hit with sugur grete plente, With fryid almondes florysshe so fre. [Liber cure cocorum (England, 1430)]

> To mak bland sorre tak the mylk of almondes blanched mad with capon brothe then tak the braun of a capon and bet it in a mortair and mele the fishe and the mylk to gedur in the mortair with the pestelle and thik it with flour of rise and boile it put ther to sugur or hony and mak it stondinge then lesk it in dyshes and diaper it with turnsole and serue it. [A Noble Boke off Cookry (England, 1468)]

As is evident from the above recipes combined with the ones below from other sources, there is a wide range of variation for this dish.

Blank Dessorre. XXXVII. Take Almandes blaunched, grynde hem and temper hem up with whyte wyne, on fleissh day with broth. and cast þerinne flour of Rys. oþer amydoun, and lye it þerwith. take brawn of Capouns yground. take sugur and salt and cast þerto and florissh it with aneys whyte. take a vessel yholes and put in safroun. and serue it forth. [Forme of Cury (England, 1390)]

Blanc desirree. Almond milk, rice flour, capon meat, sifted ginger, white sugar, white wine; each one in part to be boiled in a clean pot, and then put in the vessel in which it will be done, a little light powder; pomegranates planted thereon. [MS Royal 12.C.xii (England/France)]

Blanke desire. Take yolkes of eyron sodyn hard & safron & bred growndyn with cow milke boyl do ther to white of eyron cut smal & spyndez of porke corven ther to aley hit a lytyll with raw yolkes of eyron. [Recipes from the Wagstaff Miscellany (England, 1460)]

Blandissorye. Take almaundys, an blawnche hem, an grynde hem in a morter, an tempere hem with freysshe brothe of capoun or of beef, an swete wyne; an ȝif it be lente or fyssday, take brothe of the freysshe fysshe, an swete wyne, an boyle hem to-gederys a goode whyle; thenne take it up, an caste it on a fayre lynen clothe that is clene an drye, an draw under the clothe, wyth a ladel, alle the water that thow may fynde, ryth as thow makyst cold creme; thanne take owt of the potte, an caste it in-to a fayre potte, an let it boyle; an thanne take brawn of Capoun, an tese it smal an bray it ina morter: or ellys on a fyssday take Pyke or Elys, Codlyng or Haddok, an temper it with almaun mylke, an caste Sugre y-now ther-to; An than caste hem in-to the potte and lete hem boyle to-gederys a goode whyle: thenne take it owt of the potte alle hote, an dresse it in a dysshe, as meni don cold creme, an sette ther-on Red Anys in comfyte, or ellys Allemaundys blaunchid, an thanne serue it forth for a goode potage. [Two Fifteenth-Century Cookery-Books (England, 1430)]

45. Freschure

The unusual name of this recipe quickly leads to a similar one from *Ancient Cookery*.

> Frissure. Take hares hilt, and wasshe hom in brothe of beef with alle the blode, and boyle the blode, and skym hit wel, and then parboyle the hares, and chope hom, and frie hom in faire grees, and caste hom into a pot, and let hom boyle ensemble (together); and put therto onyons mynced, clowes, maces, pynes, and reifynges of corance, and draw up chippes of bred with wyne, and put therto; and also pouder of pepur, ande of canel, and sugre, and colour hit with saffron: ande in the fettynge doun alay (mix) hit with a lytel vynegur, and serve hit forthe. [Ancient Cookery (England, 1425)]

Given that the *Crophill* version does not specify what kind of meat is to be used, I suspect that the name "freschure" is a corruption of "fresh hare". Based on the ingredients there appear to be related recipes in both *Liber* and *Noble*.

> Harus in a sewe. Alle rawe þo hare schalle hacked be, In gobettis smalle, Syr, levys me. In hir owne blode seyn or sylud clene, Grynde brede and peper withalle bydene. Þenne temper hit with þe same bre, Þenne boyled and salted hit servyd schalle be. [Liber cure cocorum (England, 1430)]

> To mak hayres in sewe, tak a raw haire and chop hir in small gobettes and sethe hir in hir own blod thene temper it with ale pepper and bred and boile it and serue it. [A Noble Boke off Cookry (England, 1468)]

46. Apilmows de Gesse

Applemuse is one of the more common medieval recipes, so it is rather surprising that there isn't a version in *Liber* to match this one. The version in *Noble* differs from the *Crophill* in many aspects, but there is a lot of variability in apple muse overall.

> To mak an appillinose, tak appelles and sethe them and lett them kelle, then fret them throughe an heryn syff on fisshe dais take almonde mylk and oile olyf ther to. and on flesshe days tak freche brothe and whit grece and sugur and put them in a pot and boile it and colour it with saffron and cast on pouders and serue it. [A Noble Boke off Cookry (England, 1468)]

> FOR TO MAKE APULMOS. Tak Applys and seth hem and let hem kele and after mak hem thorwe a cloth and do hem im a pot and kast to that mylk of Almaundys wyth god broth of Buf in Flesch dayes do bred ymyed therto. And the fisch dayes do therto oyle of olyve and do therto sugur and colour it wyth safroun and strew theron Powder and serve it forthe. [Forme of Cury (England, 1390)]

> Apple Muse. Take Appelys an sethe hem, an Serge (Note: Sift) hem thorwe a Sefe in-to a potte; thanne take Almaunde Mylke and Hony, an caste ther-to, an gratid Brede, Safroun, Saunderys, and Salt a lytil, and caste all in the potte and lete hem sethe; and loke that thou stere it wyl, and serue it forth. [Two Fifteenth-Century Cookery-Books (England, 1430)]

47. (untitled)

This recipe is another example of a dish where the ingredients are common and there is a wide amount of variation. There is no recipe in either *Nobel* or *Liber* that corresponds directly to the one in *Crophill*, and while there are similar recipes in other medieval English cookbooks (for example, the two below), it is almost impossible to be sure if they're meant to be the same recipe or if the similarities are just a coincidence.

> TARTEE. XX.VIII. IIII. Take pork ysode. hewe it & bray it. do þerto ayrenn. Raisouns sugur and powdour of gyngur. powdour douce. and smale briddes þeramong & white grece. take prunes, safroun. & salt, and make a crust in a trape & do

þer Fars þerin. & bake it wel & serue it forth. [Forme of Cury (England, 1390)]

Tartes de chare. Take Freyssche Porke, and hew it; and grynd it in a mortere, and take it vppe in-to a fayre vesselle; and take the whyte of Eyroun and the ȝolke, y-tryid thorw a straynoure; and temper thin porke ther-with; and than take Pyneȝ, and Raysonys of Coraunce, and frye hem in Freyssche grece, and caste ther-to pouder Pepir and Gyngere, Canel, Sugre, Safroun, Salt, and caste ther-to; and do it on a cofynne, and plante the cofynne a-boue with Pruneȝ, and with Datys, and gret Roysonys of Coraunce, and smal Byrdys, or ellys harde ȝolkys of Eyroun; and yf thow tage Byrdys, frye hem in grece or thou putte hem in the cofyn; and than keuere thin cofynne; and than endore it with ȝolkys of Eyroun, and with Safroune, and late yt bake tyll it be y-now; and than serue forth. [Two Fifteenth-Century Cookery-Books (England, 1430)]

48. A Tarte Pernusames
While recipes for port and cheese tarts are fairly common in medieval sources, I could not find any matches for this recipe. The closest appears to be the following from *Forme of Cury*.

TARTES OF FLESH. XX.VIII. VIII. Take Pork ysode and grynde it smale. tarde harde eyrenn isode & ygrounde and do þerto with Chese ygronde. take gode powdour and hool spices, sugur, safroun, and salt & do þerto. make a coffyn as to feel sayde & do þis þerinne, & plaunt it with smale briddes istyned & counyng. & hewe hem to smale gobettes & bake it as tofore. & serue it forth. [Forme of Cury (England, 1390)]

49. A Tarte of Fysche
This recipe appears to be a common fish-day tart, but as with the previous recipe I could not find any clear matches. There are several recipes with similar aspects, the closest of which I've included below.

Tart for Lenton. Take figges and raisinges, and wassh hom in wyne, and grinde hom, and appuls and peres clene pared, and the corke tane out; then take fresh samon, or codlynge, or hadok, and grinde hit, and medel hit al togedur, and do hit in a coffyn, and do therto pouder of ginger, and of canelle, ande clowes, and maces; and plaunte hit above with pynes, or almondes, and prunes, and dates quartert, then cover thi coffyn, and bake hit, and serve hit forthe. [Ancient Cookery (England, 1425)]

TART DE BRYMLENT. XX.VIII. VII. Take Fyges & Raysouns. & waisshe hem in Wyne. and grinde hem smale with apples & peres clene ypiked. take hem up and cast hem in a pot wiþ wyne and sugur. take salwar Salmoun ysode. oþer codlyng, oþer haddok, & bray hem smal. & do þerto white powdours & hool spices. & salt. and seeþ it. and whanne it is sode ynowz. take it up and do it in a vessel and lat it kele. make a Coffyn an ynche depe & do þe fars þerin. Plaunt it boue with prunes and damysyns. take þe stones out, and wiþ dates quarte rede dand piked clene. and couere the coffyn, and bake it wel, and serue it forth. [Forme of Cury (England, 1390)]

Tart de ffruyte. Take figges, and seth hem in wyne, and grinde hem smale, And take hem vppe into a vessell; And take pouder peper, Canell, Clowes, Maces, pouder ginger, pynes, grete reysons of coraunce, saffron, and salte, and cast thereto; and then make faire lowe coffyns, and couche this stuff there-in, And plonte pynes aboue; and kut dates and fressh salmon in faire peces, or elles fressh eles, and parboyle hem a litull in wyne, and couche thereon; And couche the coffyns faire with the same paaste, and endore the coffyn withoute with saffron and almond mylke; and set hem in the oven and lete bake. [Two Fifteenth-Century Cookery-Books (England, 1430)]

The phrase "oyle de oyle" in the *Crophill* version is most certainly a copyist error for "oyle de olive" (olive oil).

50. Charlet
There are corresponding recipes for charlet in both *Liber* and *Noble*. In itself this isn't all that unusual as the dish appears in most of the

cookbooks from the medieval period, however the versions in *Liber*, *Noble*, and *Crophill* appear to be the only ones that include the phrase "set it down".

> Charlet. Take swettest mylke, þat þou may have, Colour hit with safron, so God þe save. Take fresshe porke and sethe hit wele, And hew hit smalle every dele. Swyng eyryn, and do þer to. Set hit over þe fyre, þenne Boyle hit and sture lest hit brenne. Whenne hit welles up, þou schalt hit kele With a litel ale, so have þou cele. When hit is inoȝe, þou sett hit doune, And kepe hit lest hit be to broune. [Liber cure cocorum (England, 1430)]

> To mak charlet tak swet mylk and colour it with saffron then tak freche pork and boile it and hew yt smalle then swinge eggs and cast them into the mylk and boile them and stirr them lest they bren and bete it with a litill ale and set it doun and let it not be brown and serue it. [A Noble Boke off Cookry (England, 1468)]

51. Ravioles
The first half of this recipe's title is unclear, with only the "R" being certain and the rest appearing to be small letters (no ascenders or descenders). The combination of "R???oles" along with the instruction to wrap the meat in pastry suggested that this is a recipe for ravioli. That being said, the recipe is not much like other contemporary English ravioli recipes.

> Raffyolys. Take swynes lire (stejh), and sethe hit, and hewe hit smalle, and do therto zolkes of egges, and medel hit wel togedur, ande make hit right fouple, ande do therto a lytel larde my need, and grated chese, and pouder of ginger, and of canelle ; then take and make balles therofas gret as an appull, and wynde hom in the calle of the swyne, every balle by hymself; then make a coffyn of paste fchapet aftur hit (formed like it), and lay hit therin, and bake hit; and when thai byn baken, take zolkes of egges, and bete hom welle in a vesscll, and do therto sugur, ande gode pouder, and colour hit with

saffron, and poure above, and serve hit forthe. [Ancient Cookery (England, 1425)]

Raynedes. Take swete porke, dates, figges, braied togeder, and put therto a fewe zolkes of eyren, and in the brayinge alay hit with a lytel brothe, and cast therto pouder of clowes, pouder of pepur, sugre, raifynges of corance, and colour hit with saffron, and medel al togeder; and then hille the stuffure in paste as men maken ruschewes; and then take the brothe of capons fothen in herbes, and let hit boyle, and colour hit with saffron, and then put in therto the raynecles, and when thai byn boyled take hom up, and lay three of hom in a dissh, and poure brothe therto; and take grated chesc medelet with pouder of ginger, and strewe above theron, and serve hit forthe. [Ancient Cookery (England, 1425)]

There is a recipe from *Liber* that seems close to the one in *Crophill*, but it is titled risshens instead.

For risshens. Take grounden porke þat soþun hase bene With peper and swongen egges clene. Put berme þer to, I undertake, As tome as belle hit wille hit make. Lay hit in a roller as sparlyng fysshe, Frye hit in grece, lay hit in dysshe. [Liber cure cocorum (England, 1430)]

52. Jussele

This simple recipe shows up in several medieval cookbooks, and the versions in *Liber*, *Noble*, and *Forme of Cury* are particularly close matches. It's interesting that among these recipes the *Noble* version is the only one that reverses the order of eggs and grated bread.

Iusselle. Take myud bred, and eyren þou swynge. Do hom togeder with out lettyng, Take fresshe broth of gode befe, Coloure hit with safron, þat is me lefe, Boyle hit softly, and in þo boylyng, Do þer to sage and persely ȝoyng. [Liber cure cocorum (England, 1430)]

To mak jusselle tak and swinge eggs and myed bred to gedur then tak freche brothe of bef and colour it with saffron and boile it softly and cast in parsley and saige and serue it. [A Noble Boke off Cookry (England, 1468)]

Jusshell. XX.II. III. Take brede ygrated and ayrenn and swyng it togydre. do þerto safroun, sawge. and salt. & cast broth. þerto. boile it & messe it forth. [Forme of Cury (England, 1390)]

53. Bokenande

As with the recipe for Jussel, Bukkenade is a fairly common dish. However the recipes in *Liber* and *Noble* are the only ones I have found that are similar to the *Crophill* verison.

Bucnade. Take almonde mylke as I con preche. Coloure hit with safron as I þe teche. Fors hit with poudur, þat is gode. Take larde of porke, wele soþyn, by þo rode. Hew hit in gobettes wele afyne. Loke þey ben smale and put hem inne. Lye hit with floure or amydone, Boyle hit wele and sett hit done. Florysshe hit with powdur, as I þe kenne, Þenne may hit be served, before gode men. [Liber cure cocorum (England, 1430)]

To mak Buknard tak almond mylk and colour it with saffron and fers it with pouder then tak lard of pork well sodene and hewe it small and put them to the mylk and alay it with flour or with amydon and boile it well and florishe it withe pouder and colour it with sanders and serue it. [A Noble Boke off Cookry (England, 1468)]

54. Blaunde Sorre

This is the second recipe for Blanc de Syre in *Crophill*, the first being recipe number 44. Interestingly, this version is much closer to the one from *Liber*.

Blonk desore. Take ryse and wasshe hom in a cup, Grynd hom smalle and temper up With almonde mylke, so have þou cele. Do hit over þo fyre and boyle hit wele. Take braune of capons or hennes alle, Hew hit þat hit be riȝt smalle. And grynd hit

wele, as myud brede, And do þer to, as I þe rede. Seson hit
with sugur grete plente, With fryid almondes florysshe so fre.
[Liber cure cocorum (England, 1430)]

55. Rosee

As with the previous recipe, there was an earlier version of Rosee
in *Crophill* (recipe number 35), and again this second version is
much closer to the recipe in *Liber*.

> Rose. Take flour of ryse, as whyte as sylke, And hit welle, with
> almond mylke. Boyle hit tyl hit be chargyd, þenne Take braune
> of capone or elle of henne. Loke þou grynd hit wondur smalle,
> And sithen þou charge hit with alle. Coloure with alkenet,
> sawnder, or ellys with blode, Fors hit with clowes or macys
> gode. Seson hit with sugur grete plenté, Þis is a rose, as kokes
> telle me. [Liber cure cocorum (England, 1430)]

56. Ynde de Cypres

The name of this recipe is a little odd. "Ynde" usually means "of
India" or possibly "indigo", and while "Indigo of Cypress" sort of
makes sense I could not find any recipes with a similar name.

The instruction to make it the same way as "blaunde sorre" does
provide an interesting clue. That recipe—number 54—includes
capon meat and almond milk, and has a close match in *Liber*.

> Blonk desore. Take ryse and wasshe hom in a cup, Grynd hom
> smalle and temper up With almonde mylke, so have þou cele.
> Do hit over þo fyre and boyle hit wele. Take braune of capons
> or hennes alle, Hew hit þat hit be riȝt smalle. And grynd hit
> wele, as myud brede, And do þer to, as I þe rede. Seson hit
> with sugur grete plente, With fryid almondes florysshe so fre.
> [Liber cure cocorum (England, 1430)]

Looking at other similar recipes from *Liber*, the following one
jumps out. It suggests that the word "Ynde" in the title may be a
copyist error for "Viande", which is sometimes spelled "vyande" in
Middle English.

Viande de Cipur. Take braunne of capons or hennes þou shalle. Parboyle and drye hit with alle. Hew hom smalle, bray in mortere, As smalle as bred, þat myed were. Take good almonde mylke anone And lye hit up with amydone Or with floure of ryse, þou may. Coloure hit with safron, I þe say. Boyle hit after yche adele, Charge hit with flesshe brayed wele. Seson hit with sugur and þen þy dysshe With almondes set þou schalle florysshe. [Liber cure cocorum (England, 1430)]

In further support for this interpretation, a version of that recipe from *Ancient Cookery* instructs the reader to color the dish with "ynde" (indigo).

Viaunde de Cypres. Take the braune of capons, and of hennes, and grynde hit smalle; and take almonde mylke made with gode brothe, and do hit in a pot, and do therto floure of ryfe, and let hit boyle; and do therto the grounden flesh, and sugur, and clowes, and maces, and colour hit wyth ynde, and let hit boyle togedur, and loke hit be stondynge, and dresse hit forthe, and almondes or paynes fryed, and styk hom right up therin. [Ancient Cookery (England, 1425)]

57. Letlardes

The title of this recipe comes from the French, "lait lardé" (larded milk). While a very common recipe in medieval English cookbooks, the versions in *Liber* and *Noble* are the closest matches.

Lede lardes. Take eyren and swete mylke of a cow, Swyng hom togedur, as I byd now. Take larde of fresshe porke with alle, Sethe hit and schere hit on peses smalle. Cast þer in and boyle hit, þenne Styr hit wele, as I þe kenne, Tyl hit be gedered on crud harde. Leche hit, and rost hit afterwarde Apone a gredel, þen serve þou may Hit forthe, with spit, as I þe say. [Liber cure cocorum (England, 1430)]

To mak ledlardes of one coloure tak eggs and cow mylk and swinge them to gedur then sethe it and hew it in small peces and boile it and stirre it till be ron upon a herd curde then lesshe it and rost it upon a gredirn and serue it [A Noble Boke off Cookry (England, 1468)]

58. Botre of Almaunde Melk

There are versions of this recipe in both *Liber* and *Noble*. The *Liber* version uses the phrase "a mile away", making the corresponding text in the *Crophill* version more understandable.

> Buttur of Almonde mylke. Take thykke mylke of almondes clere, Boyle wele alle in fere. And in þo boylyng, cast þerinne Venegur, oþer ellys gode wyne. Do hit soþenne in a canvas þenne, In soþun, gar hit on hepe to renne. In clothe þou henge hit a myle way, And after in colde water þou hit lay. Serve hit forthe in þe dysshe, Þat day þo lorde is servyd with fysshe. [Liber cure cocorum (England, 1430)]

I still can't work out the origin of the cryptic title for the *Noble* version. If it's a copyist error then it's quite an impressive one.

> To mak Z S. V tak thik almond mylke and boile it and in the boilinge cast in wyne or venygar and put it in a canvas and let it ren on a hepe then honge it in a clothe and lay it in cold water and serue it. [A Noble Boke off Cookry (England, 1468)]

59. Charlet Aforce

While there are a number of versions of this recipe in other sources, the closest match is from *Noble*.

> To mak charlet forced tak cowe mylk and yolks of eggs draw throughe a stren and bet it to gedur then tak freshe pork smalle hewene and cast all to gedure in a pan and colour it with saffrone and let it boile till it be on a crud then take it up and lay it on a clothe upon a bord and presse out the whey then tak the mylk of almondes or cow creme and sett it on the fyere put ther to sugur and colour it depe with saffrone then leshe out the crud and couche it in dishes and pour out the ceripe and cast on sugur and canelle and serve it. [A Noble Boke off Cookry (England, 1468)]

60. Farsure

The closest match for this recipe appears to be the following one from *Ancient Cookery*.

> Farsure for chekyns. Take fressh porke, and fethe hit, and hew hit smal, and grinde hit wel; and put therto harde zolkes of egges, and medel hom wel togedur, and do therto raifynges of corance, and pouder of cancl, and maces, and quibibz (cubebs), and of clowes al hole; and colour hit with saffron, and do hit into the chekyns; and then parboyle hom, and roste, and endore (baste) hom with rawc zolkes of egges, and fiaume hom if hit be nede, and serve hit forthe. [Ancient Cookery (England, 1425)]

61. Farsure For Soper

Like the previous recipe, the only close match for this one is from *Ancient Cookery*.

> Farsure for chekins. Take the zolkes of harde egges, and bray hom smal, and take fauge and parsel and hew hit smal, and medel (mingle) hom wel togedur, and do therto raisynges of corance, and pouder of canel, and pouder of ginger, and do into the chekyns, and parboyle hom, and roste hom, and do as I faide tofore. [Ancient Cookery (England, 1425)]

62. Char de Marchaunt

This recipe is one of the few cases where there is a match in *Noble* without a corresponding one in *Liber*.

> For To Mak Charmarchaunt. Tak restes of motton choped and put them in a faire pot and set them on the fier with clene water and boile it welle then take parsley and saige and bete it in a mortair with bred and draw it up to the brothe and put it in the pot with the flesh and let it sethe to gedure and salt it and serve it furthe. [A Noble Boke off Cookry (England, 1468)]

63. Powmes Dorre

There are versions of pommes dorry in both *Liber* and *Noble*, but neither is a close match for the *Crophill* version. This may not be surprising given the wide amount of variability for the recipe in medieval English sources.

For powme dorrys. Take porke and grynde hit rawe, I kenne, Temper hit with swongen egges. þenne Kast powder to make hit on a balle. In playand water þou kast hit schalle To harden, þenne up þou take, Enbroche hit fayre for goddes sake. Endore hit with ȝolkes of egges þen With a fedyr at fyre, as I þe kenne. Bothe grene and rede þow may hit make With iuse of herbȝ I undertake. Halde under a dysshe þat noȝt be lost, More honest hit is as þou wele wost. [Liber cure cocorum (England, 1430)]

To mak pomes tak and grind raw pork and temper them with swonge egges caft ther to good poudurs and [quere, rolle omitted?] it in a balle and lay it in boillinge water to hardyn then tak it up and endore it with yolks of eggs and ye may make it grene or red with juce of erbes and serue it. [A Noble Boke off Cookry (England, 1468)]

XLII - FOR TO MAKE POMMEDORRY. Tak Buff and hewe yt smal al raw and cast yt in a morter and grynd yt nozt to smal tak safroun and grynd therewyth wan yt ys grounde tak the wyte of the eyryn zyf yt be nozt styf. Cast into the Buf pouder of Pepyr olde resyns and of coronse set over a panne wyth fayr water and mak pelotys of the Buf and wan the water and the pelots ys wel yboylyd and set yt adoun and kele yt and put yt on a broche and rost yt and endorre yt wyth zolkys of eyryn and serve yt forthe. [Forme of Cury (England, 1390)]

xix - Pome dorres. Take Fylettys of Raw porke, and grynd hem wyl; do Salt and pouder Pepir ther-to; than take the Whyte of the Eyroun andthrow ther-to, and make hem so hard that they mow ben Rosted on a Spete; make hem round as an Appil: make fyre with-owte smoke; then take Almaunde mylke, and ybontyd flour, do hem to-gederys; take Sugre, and putte in thin bature; then dore hem with sum grene thing, percely or ȝolkys of Eyroun, to-geder, that they ben grene; and be wyl war that they ben nowt Browne; and sum men boyle hem in freysshe broth or they ben spetid; and whan they ben so boylid, then they must ben sette an kelid, and than Spete hem, and dore hem with ȝolkys of Eyroun y-mengyd with the Ius of haselle leuys. [Two Fifteenth-Century Cookery-Books (England, 1430)]

64. Brewet Sechz

This snippet of a recipe does not have a match in either *Liber* or *Noble*. There are other recipes for "Brewet Sechz", but they all seem to be related in name only.

Browet sek. Sweet broth, grape verjuice, ground parsley put therein, cloves, mace, cubebs; in times of chicks after Easter; and it will have the taste of good spices, saffron cooked therein with parsley in the broth; color, yellow. [MS Royal 12.C.xii (England/France]

Cxiij - Bruette saake. Take Capoun, skalde hem, draw hem, smyte hem to gobettys, Waysshe hem, do hem in a potte; thenne caste owt the potte, waysshe hem a-ȝen on the potte, and caste ther-to half wyne half Brothe; take Percely, Isope, Waysshe hem, and hew hem smal, and putte on the potte ther the Fleysshe is; caste ther-to Clowys, quybibes, Maces, Datys y-tallyd, hol Safroune; do it ouer the fyre; take Canelle, Gyngere, tempere thin powajes with wyne; caste in-to the potte Salt ther-to, hele (Note: Cover) it, and whan it is y-now, serue it forth. [Two Fifteenth-Century Cookery-Books (England, 1430)]

65. Brewet of Elys

There are recipes for brewet of eels in both *Liber* and *Noble*, though the ingredients differ and the instructions have significantly more detail than the *Crophill* version.

To mak eles in bruet tak eles culpond and boile them with mynced onyons padley and saige and draw it with whit bred and wyne put ther to pouder of pepper canelle and salt and serue it. [A Noble Boke off Cookry (England, 1468)]

For a brothe of elys. Fyrst flyghe þyn elys, in pese hom smyte, Put hom in pot, þagh þay ben lyte, With clene water. þen take þou schalle Alle powder of peper, coloure hit with alle With safroune and alyed þenne With floure, and cast alle in, I kenne, At þe fyrst boylyng þat may falle Soth hote, and serve hit in to þe halle. [Liber cure cocorum (England, 1430)]

66. Browet of Lamprouns
While recipes for lampreys show up in many medieval English cookbooks, there aren't many. The recipes for brewet of lampreys in *Liber*, *Noble*, and *Forme of Cury* all seem to me more closely related to each other than to the *Crophill* version.

Lamprayes in browet. Take lamprayes and scalde hom by kynde, Sythyn, rost hom on gredyl, and grynde Peper and safrone. welle hit with alle, Do þo lampreyes and serve hit in sale. [Liber cure cocorum (England, 1430)]

To mak a Lampry in bruet tak a lampry and skald hym and rost hym on a gredirn then grind pepper guingere clowes and saffron and sethe it well and put pepper in the lampry and serue it. [A Noble Boke off Cookry (England, 1468)]

XI - FOR TO MAKE LAMPREYS IN BRUET. They schulle be schaldyd and ysode and ybrulyd upon a gredern and grynd peper and safroun and do ther'to and boyle it and do the Lomprey ther'yn and serve yt forth. [Forme of Cury (England, 1390)]

67. Perre
This recipe appears to be unique in medieval English sources. There are a couple of contemporary German recipes that include

both pears and poultry, but they both differ widely in terms of the rest of the ingredients and instructions.

68. Maumene
There are a large number of recipes for mawmeney, including the versions in *Liber* and *Noble*. While the ingredients and instructions vary widely from source to source, the *Crophill* version appears to be the only one that includes figs and raisins.

> For to make momene. Take whyte wyne, I telle þe, And sugur þerto ry3t grete plenté. Take, bray þo brawne of a3t capon. To a pot of oyle of on galon, And of hony a qwharte þou take. Do hit þer to as ever þou wake, Take powder þo mountenaunce of a pownde, And galingale ginger and canel rownde, And cast þer to, and styre hit. þenne Alle in on pot sethe hit, I kenne. [Liber cure cocorum (England, 1430)]

> To mak mamony, tak whit wyne and sugur then bray the braun of viii capons with a gal on of oile and a quart of hony put ther to poudur of pepper galingalle guingere and canelle and stirre it welle and serue it. [A Noble Boke off Cookry (England, 1468)]

69. Kokeneye
I could not find any other versions of this recipe. The text cuts off abruptly in the manuscript, with the last word written by itself near the center of the bottom margin, so it could be that there was more and that the full recipe might resemble something from another book. As it is, the few ingredients and the title offer little help.

One possibility is the recipe for "comyne sewe" from *Liber*. It starts similarly (albeit with veal instead of poultry) and the title is close enough to be a copyist error, but there are enough differences that any similarities could just be a coincidence.

> For comyne sewe. 3iff þou wylle make a comyne sew, Vele and motun and porke þou hew On smalle gobettis. put hom in pot With mynsud onyons, ful wele I wot, And powder of Peper þou kast þerto. Coloure hit with safroune or þou more do,

And draw3e alyoure of browne crust eke To alye þis sew þat is so meke. [Liber cure cocorum (England, 1430)]

Of the 69 recipes in the *John Crophill's Commonplace Book*, 34 have a corresponding recipe in *Liber cure cocorum*. Additionally, there are short sequences of recipes that appear in both sources in roughly the same order. While this suggests the two cookbooks are related, I have not been able to determine if one was a source for the other or if both drew from a common source.

The table below lists all of the *Crophill* recipes along with the corresponding recipe from *Liber* when possible.

1. A Tarte of Fysch .... [ ]
2. Browet of Almayne .... 17. Breuet De almond
3. Furmente .... 4. Furmente
4. Blamanger .... 10. Blonc Manger
5. Chaudon Sauz of Swannes ...... 69. Sawce For Swannus
6. Amydone .... 5. Amydone
7. Conyes in Grave .... 6. Conyngus in Gravé
8. Chikens in Cryteyne .... 7. Chekyns in Cretene
9. Viaunde de Cipre .... 8. Viande de Cipur
10. Maretrel de le Char .... 9. Mortrews de Chare
11. Chaudone Potage of Pygys ... 11. Þandon for Wylde Digges
12. Browes de Chaudoun .... [ ]
13. Noumbles of Net .... 13. Nombuls
14. Roo in Sewe .... 51. Roo in a Sewe
15. Counsis .... 53. Capons in Covisye
16. Let Lorres des Aguellys .... [ ]
17. Cherise .... [ ]
18. Soppes Dorre .... 24. Sowpus Dorre
19. Blawmanger of Lekys .... 107. Blaunchyd Porray
20. Browet of Almayne .... 17. Breuet de Almonde
21. Rys Rayle .... [ ]
22. Pochee .... 104. Figge
23. Browet Mese .... [ ]
24. Crane .... [ ]
25. Charlet Gentyl .... [ ]
26. Viaunde de Cipre .... 8. Viande de Cipur
27. Viaunde de Burgeoun .... [ ]
28. Burgeoun de Vyne .... [ ]
29. Rys Camelyne .... [ ]
30. A Stywe .... [ ]

GLOSSARY

amidon (also: amydon, amydone) - Wheat starch.

ayren (also: ayron, eyren, eyroun, eyryn) - Eggs, from the German "eier".

brawn (also: braun, braune) - Flesh. The term is typically only applied to meat.

canell (also: canel, canelle) - Cassia (*Cinnamomum cassia* - Sold as "cinnamon" in the United States). Possibly cinnamon (*Cinnamomum zeylenicum*) as well.

caudle (also: caudell) - A smooth, thick soup or beverage, usually made with eggs.

chargaunt (also: chargeaunt) - Very thick. Chargeant seems to be somewhere between "thick" and "stonding" in consistency.

chewett (also: chauet) -

civey (also: cyve) - Meat gravy, typically made with onions.

culpon (also: culpouns) - Slices or shreds of meat.

damacyns (also: damsons) - Plums.

dight (also: dyght, dyghte) - To carve. The term is typically used for game birds.

eysel - Cider vinegar.

farced - Stuffed.

galentyn - A sauce for meats, usually made with the juice of the meat thickened with bread crumbs.

galingale (also: galyngale) - Lesser Galingale (*Alpinia officinarum*), a member of the ginger family.

gelofres - Gillyflower. An old-world plant with scented flowers, sometimes used as a substitute for cloves.

greyn de pareys - Grains of Paradise (*Aframomum melegueta*), also known as Guinea pepper or Melegueta pepper.

humbles (also numbelys, umbelys) - Entrails, usually the kidneys.

lesh (also lesche, lesche) - To slice, or a slice.

lyre - The muscle of the thigh. Also, a mix of bread and a liquid, usually broth or wine, used as a sauce (a corruption of "liquor").

meddle - To mix.

menge - To mix.

mortrues - A dish of pounded or ground meat.

numbles (also nombles, nomblys, humbles) - Entrails, usually the kidneys.

osey - A type of sweet wine, possibly from France or Portugal.

qwybibes - Cubebs (*Piper cubeba*). A type of pepper with a citrus-like scent. Also called Tailed Pepper.

saunders - Powdered red sandalwood (*Pterocarpus santalinus*), used as a colorant.

seethe (also: sithe, sothen, soden) - Boil, boiled.

stondyng - Extremely thick, like thick oatmeal (lit. "standing").

swyng - To beat or whip.

temper (also: temper) - Mix, blend, balance.

turnsol - A number of plants of the genus Heliotropium, used to produce red, purple, or blue colors.

umbles - See "numbles"

BIBLIOGRAPHY

Austin, Thomas. *Two Fifteenth-century Cookery-books. Harleian Ms. 279 (ab. 1430), & Harl. Ms. 4016 (ab. 1450), with Extracts from Ashmole Ms. 1429, Laud Ms. 553, & Douce Ms. 55*. London: Pub. for the Early English Text Society by N. Trübner &, 1888. Print.

Cotgrave, R. *A Dictionarie of the French and English Tongues*. London: Printed by A. Islip, 1611. Print.

Hieatt, C. "Middle English culinary recipes in MS Harley 5401". Medium Aevum 65, 1996, 54-71.

Hinson, J. "Le Menagier de Paris." *Le Menagier de Paris*. Recreational Medievalism. Web. 20 November, 2015.

Mayhew, Anthony Lawson., and Walter William. Skeat. *A Concise Dictionary of Middle English: From A.D. 1150 to 1580*. Oxford: At the Clarendon, 1888. Print.

Morris, Richard. *Liber Cure Cocorum*. Berlin: Published for the Philological Society by A. Asher &, 1862. Print.

Myers, Daniel. "Enseignements." *Enseignements*. Medieval Cookery, 2005. Web. 28 May 2013.

Myers, Daniel. "British Library MS Royal 12.C.xii." *MS Royal 12.C.xii*. Medieval Cookery, 19 Jan. 2012. Web. 30 Nov. 2015.

Myers, Daniel. Recipes from the Wagstaff Miscellany. N.p.: Blackspoon, 2015. Print.

Napier, Robina. *A Noble Boke off Cookry*. Lond.: Elliot Stock, 1882. Print.

Pegge, Samuel, Richard, and Gustavus Brander. *The Forme of Cury: A Roll of Ancient English Cookery, Compiled, about A.D. 1390, by the Master-cooks of ... Richard II ... and Now in the Possession of Gustavus Brander, Esq.* London: J. Nichols, 1780. Print.

Warner, Richard. *Antiquitates Culinariae = or Curious Tracts Relating to the Culinary Affairs of the Old English*. N.p.: Printed for R. Blamire, 1791. Print.

www.ingramcontent.com/pod-product-compliance
Lightning Source LLC
Chambersburg PA
CBHW071841020426
42331CB00007B/1806